OHAVI ZEDEK SYNAGOGUE LIBRARY
188 NORTH PROSPECT STREET
BURLINGTON, VERMONT 05401
(802) 864-0218

D0216473

3364

HALIVNI,
DAVID W.

"REVELATION
RESTORED"

220.10
HAL

Revelation Restored

RADICAL
TRADITIONS

THEOLOGY IN A POSTCRITICAL KEY

Series Editors: Stanley M. Hauerwas, Duke University, and Peter Ochs, University of Virginia

BOOKS IN THE SERIES:

Wilderness Wanderings: Probing Twentieth-Century Theology and Philosophy, *Stanley M. Hauerwas*

Revelation Restored: Divine Writ and Critical Responses, *David Weiss Halivni*

Radical Traditions cuts new lines of inquiry across a confused and confusing array of debates concerning the place of theology in modernity and, more generally, the status and role of scriptural faith in contemporary life. Charged with a rejuvenated confidence, spawned in part by the rediscovery of reason as inescapably tradition constituted, a new generation of theologians and religious scholars is returning to scriptural traditions with the hope of retrieving resources long ignored, depreciated, and in many cases ideologically suppressed by modern habits of thought. *Radical Traditions* assembles a promising matrix of strategies, disciplines, and lines of thought that invites Jewish, Christian, and Islamic theologians back to the word, recovering and articulating modes of scriptural reasoning as that which always underlies modernist reasoning and therefore has the capacity—and authority—to correct it.

Far from despairing over modernity's failings, postcritical theologies rediscover resources for renewal and self-correction within the disciplines of academic study themselves. Postcritical theologies open up the possibility of participating once again in the living relationship that binds together God, text, and community of interpretation. *Radical Traditions* thus advocates a "return to the text," which means a commitment to displaying the richness and wisdom of traditions that are at once text based, hermeneutical, and oriented to communal practice.

Books in this series offer the opportunity to speak openly with practitioners of other faiths or even with those who profess no (or limited) faith, both academics and nonacademics, about the ways religious traditions address pivotal issues of the day. Unfettered by foundationalist preoccupations, these books represent a call for new paradigms of reason—a thinking and rationality that is more responsive than originative. By embracing a postcritical posture, they are able to speak unapologetically out of scriptural traditions manifest in the practices of believing communities (Jewish, Christian, and others); articulate those practices through disciplines of philosophic, textual, and cultural criticism; and engage intellectual, social, and political practices that for too long have been insulated from theological evaluation. *Radical Traditions* is radical not only in its confidence in nonapologetic theological speech but also in how the practice of such speech challenges the current social and political arrangements of modernity.

Revelation Restored

DIVINE WRIT AND CRITICAL RESPONSES

David Weiss Halivni

WestviewPress

A Division of HarperCollins*Publishers*

Radical Traditions: Theology in a Postcritical Key

All rights reserved. Printed in the United States of America. No part of this publication may be reproduced or transmitted in any form or by any means, electronic or mechanical, including photocopy, recording, or any information storage and retrieval system, without permission in writing from the publisher.

Copyright © 1997 by David Weiss Halivni

Published in 1997 in the United States of America by Westview Press, 5500 Central Avenue, Boulder, Colorado 80301-2877, and in the United Kingdom by Westview Press, 12 Hid's Copse Road, Cumnor Hill, Oxford OX2 9JJ

Library of Congress Cataloging-in-Publication Data
Halivni, David.
   Revelation restored : divine writ and critical responses
/ David Weiss Halivni.
      p.   cm. — (Radical traditions)
   Includes bibliographical references and index.
   ISBN 0-8133-3346-6
   1. Bible. O.T. Pentateuch—Canon.   2. Bible. O.T. Pentateuch—
Criticism, interpretation, etc., Jewish .   3. Bible. O.T.
Pentateuch—Hermeneutics.   I. Title.   II. Series.
BS1225.2.C85   1997
222'.101—dc21   97-8573
                                                                                  CIP
                                                                                  r972

The paper used in this publication meets the requirements of the American National Standard for Permanence of Paper for Printed Library Materials Z39.48-1984.

10   9   8   7   6   5   4   3   2

For Avidan and those who will follow him.
My first grandchild—a sense of continuity.

Contents

Ezra-Cassiodorus figure from the Codex Amiatinus.

Foreword:
Revelation Restored
as Postcritical Theology

PETER OCHS, SERIES COEDITOR

David Weiss Halivni makes the priestly and prophetic scribe Ezra the hero of his *Revelation Restored:* As redactor and teacher of the *Torah she-bichtav,* "the written Torah," to the people Israel after the First Destruction, Ezra rescues his people from ignorance of Torah and thus separation from God. We find no better way to introduce Westview Press's new book series, "Radical Traditions: Theology in a Postcritical Key." For Ezra the Scribe is not only pivotal in the history of retrieving and renewing ancient Israelite religious history; he stands also as a representative figure for the series of scribal sages whose restorative work links the founding traditions of Judaism, Christianity, and Islam to the work of postcritical theologians today. In the shadow of *Shoah* (the Hebrew term for "Holocaust," "utter destruction and desolation") and after the demise of the imperialistic discourses of western secularism, the task of postcritical theologians is at once to restore and to re-form the foundational discourses of the Abrahamite traditions—the sacred Scriptures and the primordial commentaries that gave them life in the founding communities and in the receiving communities that serve the One God. The projected goal of postcritical theology is to retrieve, correct, and restore these foundational discourses as first principles, not only of our community-specific theologies, but also of western academic inquiry.

As a restorative inquiry, postcritical theology recognizes, to be sure, that these discourses are also self-reforming. As a reformatory inquiry, however, postcritical theology also acknowledges that the humanistic projects of the Renaissance and Enlightenment were not mere errors. They were stimulated by legitimate doubts about the capacities of late medieval or scholastic practices to meet the challenges of new industrial, scientific, and political realities. The uncompromising character of humanistic, or "Cartesian," doubt is in fact an index of the scriptural traditions' own capacity for infinite criticism: that searing negation that the wholly infinite God of Israel, alone, engenders. Renaissance and Enlightenment humanisms failed only because they detached this negation from its source and, thereby, from the traditions of Scripture and commentary that should have remained the ever-renewing and renewable sources rather than the objects of humanistic criticism. Postcritical theology restores the Abrahamite resources of western humanism and then undertakes its critical task of reforming both academic and theological inquiries from out of these resources. The postcritical return to Scripture is, therefore, not triumphalistic, nor is it antimodern or antiacademic; acknowledging the failings of both medieval and modern practices of Abrahamite religion, it reenlists the discourses of the modern academy as *instruments* of the perennial, scriptural reformation of religious as well as academic inquiry.

For the series *Radical Traditions,* Ezra the Scribe is therefore a figure, as well, for the rabbinic sages who save, teach, and reinterpret the Torah after the Destruction of the Second Temple; for the sages of the Early Church who, on the model of Jerome, begin to write as well as speak their own transcriptions, translations, and interpretations of the story of the One who was crucified and resurrected for the sake of human redemption; for the sages of the foundational narrative and legal texts of early Islam (the literatures of *haddit* and *sharia*) who receive, transmit, and comment on the teachings of the Koran; and for the successive generations of sages whose efforts link these founding literatures to the work of contemporary postcritical theology. The figure of Ezra in Halivni's work therefore complements the icon we have adopted for this series of books: the image of a scribe who may be identified, ambiguously, as Ezra or as Jerome or as Cassiodorus or, later, as Erasmus the religious humanist. These all serve as models for the works of our series authors, beginning with Halivni.

Lucius N. Littauer Professor of classical Jewish civilization at Columbia University, cofounder and rector of the Institute of Traditional Judaism in Teaneck, New Jersey, and former head of the Talmud Department of the Jewish Theological Seminary, Halivni is this century's most innovative Talmudist. Until his recent project of writing theological and hermeneutical studies in English, he was widely known only among sophisticated readers of his ongoing magnum opus, *Mekorot uMesorot (Sources and Traditions).*[1] For nonspecialists in Talmud, this central corpus of Halivni's work is distant: a highly technical, wondrous play of hypothetical reconstructions of the text's history of redaction.[2] In *Revelation Restored,* he completes a series of English-language studies that articulate the theological and hermeneutical implications of these reconstructions for a broader, contemporary public.

For Halivni, Ezra's work rescues the Torah both from oblivion and from its own acquired blemishes. This "rescue from oblivion" is a theme of the books of Ezra and Nehemiah in their plain sense:

Ezra came up from Babylon, a scribe expert in the Teaching of Moses which
the Lord God of Israel had given. (Ezra 7:6)

On the first day of the seventh month, Ezra the priest brought the Teaching
before the congregation. . . . He read from it . . . to the men and women and
those who could understand. . . . Ezra the scribe stood upon a wooden tower
made for the purpose .. . . Jeshua, Bani, . . . and the Levites explained the
Teaching to the people. . . . They read from the scroll of the Teaching of God,
translating it and giving the sense; so they understood the reading. (Nehemiah
8: 2–7)

"Rescuing the Torah from its own acquired blemishes" is not an explicit theme, but one that Halivni derives from a Talmudic tradition and
adopts as a way of intrepreting the written Torah in its nonliteral, or
midrashic, sense. The Talmudic tradition is, as indicated explicitly in the
books of Kings, that the children of Israel sinned, *chate'u yisrael,* which
means that they did not always maintain the Temple or the Torah scrolls it
contained or the teachings contained within them. Halivni reasons that if
Israel did not properly maintain the Torah, then there is no reason to assume that the Torah text and traditions were correctly transmitted
through the period of the Kings to Ezra. The implication of this assumption is that Ezra received what Halivni terms "the maculate Torah": a not-
immaculate statement of God's words. As suggested by several Talmudic
passages, and as articulated by Halivni, Ezra worked under divine inspiration to correct what words of this maculate text he had time and occasion
to correct, to mark (with *puncta extraordinaria,* or *nekudot*) errant texts
whose correct readings were preserved orally, and otherwise to leave oral
instructions about how the remaining errant teachings should be corrected. These instructions constitute a part of the *Torah she-b'al-peh,* or
the oral Torah: the living Torah that, according to chapter 1 of *Mishnah
Avot* (Sayings of the Fathers), was handed down from Moses to Joshua,
through elders and priests, to the rabbinic sages and then exhibited in the
Mishnah, the Talmuds, the midrash, and the ongoing literature that interprets them.

Since this rabbinic literature appears only after the Second Destruction,
Halivni's readers may want to draw analogies between Ezra's restoring the
written Torah after the fires of the First Destruction and the rabbinic sages'
restoring the oral Torah after the fires of the second. Two Judaisms saved
from the fire. Those who have read Halivni's recent Holocaust memoir,
*The Book and the Sword: A Life of Learning in the Shadow of
Destruction,*[3] may also want to extend the analogies to Halivni's own
work. Here, in the shadow of *Shoah,* Halivni writes how a certain kind of
Talmudic study has kept him in life:

Anyone whose lungs absorbed, on the ramp, on the station platform of
Auschwitz, the smoke effusing from the chimneys of the crematoria . . . these
are different people who have known a different kind of abandonment. . . . A
sensitive survivor . . . should work under the influence of mutually contradictory forces. . . . On the one hand, one must find fault with what happened, for
if there is no fault, there is an indirect affirmation. . . . On the other hand, if
you acknowledge the wrong, then you run the risk of cutting off the branch
upon which you rest. A sensitive theologian must work with both sides, for if
you take away the tradition, too, you take away the branch upon which you
were raised and nurtured. . . .

Personally, I found this balance in the critical study of Jewish texts, in a
combination of criticism and belief in the divine origin of the text. My studies
often question the veracity of the text as we find it, and at the same time they
aim to increase the dignity of this text by restoring earlier readings. . . .

This contradiction is not unlike the one that began to bother me in child-
hood and still troubles me. Once I wrote: "How is one to explain the blatant
contradiction between counting and upholding every word, every letter of the
text, and at the same time boldly pronouncing, '*Chasora mechasra vehacha
ketanti*'—'There is a lacuna in the text, and it should be read differently'?"
The Rabbis had to lend divine power to the text to lend power to their defi-
ance of it. A lacuna in a human text is of no religious significance. A lacuna in
a divine text? That already smacks of heresy. The Rabbis of the Talmud tam-
pered with the biblical text, frequently offered interpretations that ran counter
to the integrity of it, and openly said: There is a lacuna in the Mishnah. . . .

As religious Jews, we have to know that without God there is no humanity.
. . . It's like a trolley car . . . : you may think the conductor is in charge, but the
power comes from above. "Walk humbly with the Lord thy God" (Micah
6:8)—like a child holding hands. *You must hold hands, and walk.* But this
does not mean that you always have to say, particularly in remembrance of
the Holocaust, "What you did was right." It was terribly wrong.[4]

Like Ezra and like the rabbinic sages, Halivni writes after destruction
and writes at once to restore and to criticize and restate the Torah that he
has received. Giving voice to a Talmudic tradition, Halivni calls this a maculate Torah, but one whose holiness inheres in its "maculation," for it is
through the repair of this text that the scribe, sage, or scholar enters into
intimate relation with its divine author. The divine author says, "I will be
with you in suffering"; the suffering is here, too, in the text, and the possibility of repair, *tikkun*, when the repair of the maculate text also means repair of the maculate world, *tikkun olam.*

The frontispiece for this book is therefore a scribe whose work is dedi-
cated to healing divine text as well as human texts and human person and
human community. The idea for this icon was suggested by a lecture Mark

Vessey delivered at Drew University in March 1997. Paraphrasing an essay by Paul Meyvaert, Vessey notes that the image of a scribe placed

> at the beginning of the Codex Amiatinus, and produced around 700 C.E. at Bede's monastery of Wearmouth-Jarrow in Northumbria, is the first extant representation of Ezra in Christian art. The image derives from a similar portrait in an Italian pandect of the Bible, produced in the monastery of Vivarium (Calabria) under the direction of Cassiodorus, Roman statesman turned patron and instructor of monks, in the second half of the sixth century. Mayvaert now argues that Cassiodorus' Bible did *not* show Ezra at all but simply a late Roman, Christian scribe or man of letters, busy writing (transcribing) a biblical text. Cassiodorus may have intended this figure as a self-portrait, but the monks of Wearmouth-Jarrow had no means of recognizing him as the person depicted. Instead, probably on the suggestion of Bede, they travestied the portrait as one of Ezra, completing it with the accoutrements of a Jewish high priest! A couplet over the Amiatinus image runs: "Codicibus sacris hostili clade perustis / Esda Deo fervens hoc reparavit opus" ("When the sacred books had been consumed in the fires of war, Ezra, inspired by God, restored this work"). Mayvaert shows how Bede developed his vision of Ezra's scribal activity in his commentaries, mostly on the basis of 4 Esdras.[5]

The interpretive history of this image is as pertinent to the series *Radical Traditions* as is its content: the image of a Roman orator *reinterpreted in light of a scriptural theology* as the Hebrew scribe who, in turn, reinterpreted the written Torah, once singed by the fires of war, in order to *restore* its text and meaning. Vessey adds his own imaginative reading to the story. Completing the iconic circle that links together the scriptural and humanistic elements of our contemporary theological practice, he speculates that the prototype for Bede's rereading was an image of St. Jerome in his study, writing his own biblical commentary after the model of Ezra, and that this served, as well, as prototype for the better-known images of Erasmus, the religious humanist, at his own desk, writing in the manner of Christian–biblical scribe. Vessey plans to, but has not yet tested, his reading against the historical record. This fact, itself, contributes to our image of postcritical theology: an icon of the theologically grounded historical scholar's capacity to imagine beyond the limits of explicit, historical documentation, not to supplant history, but in ways consistent with but not reducible to the explicit documentation, to deepen our expectations of what history may reveal.

One of the central concerns of postcritical theology is, in fact, to redress the modern academy's tendency to reduce religious history to the terms of a single variety of empiricist historiography. In *Revelation Restored*, Halivni calls this the kind of history that refers only to certain "factual events as best as these may be established from the evidence [of ancient texts]." To articulate Halivni's approach, we might label this "plain-sense historiography," to be distinguished from a "depth historiography" that discloses what Halivni calls a "transcendent history" that "is more than the sum total of the events recorded." Halivni's postcritical innovation is, through such a depth historiography, to bring plain-sense history into dialogue with "theological reading," which, in turn, draws the religious practices and theological concerns of the receiving community into dialogue with those of the community under study.

The key to understanding Halivni's work is not to reduce depth history to either plain sense history or theology alone. "Plain sense historiography" refers to the attempt to disclose precisely what kind of overt human behaviors lay behind the biblical and rabbinic texts: what any of us would have seen if we were there. If Halivni's thesis about Ezra belonged only to this kind of historiography, then it would be simply an ostensive claim about how one man restored the literal meaning of what God actually said to Moses on Mount Sinai. In this case, the corrected oral Torah that Ezra initiated would function just the way the plain sense text was supposed to function and there would be, in fact, only one genre of text, not two. However, Halivni's claim should not be understood as "confessional theology," defined as the attempt to show what meaning the biblical or rabbinic community's textual claims would have for the life and thought of the contemporary religious community. If his thesis about Ezra were merely theological in this sense, then it could not be falsified by the evidence of the sacred texts themselves or of sound historiographic scholarship; his thesis would, conversely, make no claim on historical or literary scholars. In this case, there would be no way to distinguish Ezra's activity from the oral Torah of the rabbinic sages who make claims about him, and once again, the oral Torah the rabbis received could not be distinguished from the written Torah Ezra received.

Halivni's depth historiography draws on the resources of both plain sense history and theology but adds to them the mediatory and interpretive judgments that, alone, add the theological depth missing from empiricist histories, the evidentiary rules missing from ahistorical theologies, and the devout rationality present only when disciplined scholarship and theology meet. This mediation is won at the price of either deductive or inductive certainty. Depth historiography has the modality of a hypothesis, or "abduction" in Charles Peirce's terms—it is subject to falsification and to more precise definition—but it offers the kinds of hypotheses on which, as Peirce says, after Pascal, people can wager their lives. In Halivni's practice, depth historiography is a response to lacunae in the explicit documentary evidence. The biblical and historiographic documents do not, for example, account fully for what Ezra was doing when he "brought the Teaching before the congregation." That is an issue of critical importance to the lives of those who live by the Bible, but the evidence is incomplete and incompletable. Out of concern for their religious communities, confessional theologians might, nonetheless, fashion an account that would underwrite certain contemporary behaviors: the way the Talmudic sages might, for example, portray Abraham as having worn tefillin. Critical of such eisegesis, plain sense historiographers would have any of three alternatives to offer: to promote a single reading disingenuously as if it were necessitated by the documentation; simply to speculate on the range of options that would be logically possible, or, agnostically, to disclaim our capacity to know anything beyond the explicit evidence.

If history were written to serve the function, exclusively, of intellectual clarification, either of the latter two options might be taken. If, however, history provides a foundation for making judgments about how we live our lives, then such intellectual distance is inadequate and we need to eliminate the first and third options. The first option is simply deceitful. As illustrated in Julius Wellhausen's claims about the lateness of the priestly documents, this first option is often taken when theologically interested historians choose to make ostensibly documentary claims on the basis of unexplicated theological predispositions. Such scholars as Yehezkiel Kaufmann, Moshe Greenberg, and John Levinson have exhibited the error and disingenuousness of this aspect of Wellhausen's work and, by implication, of other work like it.[6]

However, the third alternative, pleading agnosticism, will also not suffice, since decisions about contemporary practice have to be made, evidence or not. The second alternative makes a necessary contribution to any and all proper theological readings of history. We must ask what range of possible readings are warranted by the historical-documentary evidence in its plain sense. Then, however, we must also choose among them. In Halivni's case, that is to suggest which reading would best explain a given text in light of the historiographic evidence, interpreted in response to the religious needs of the day and in the context of the contemporary theologian's broadest understanding of the community's tradition of text reading and religious practice. The kind of depth history Halivni thereby offers cannot be reduced to the least common denominator of some historiographic or literary method; this judgment relies on the person who makes it. It is no merely subjective judgment, however, because not just anyone can make it, but only one whose inquiry emerges out of exhaustive familiarity with text and tradition and religious life *and* whose reading will capture the attention and commitment of a receiving community of scholar-practitioners. It is, in sum, a *fallible,* theological judgment founded on historical and literary study, which illuminates history at the point where evidence goes no further and which serves at the same time to resolve a sig-

nificant problem in the life of a contemporary community of scholar/prac-
titioners.

Through the way it resolves this problem, depth history also discloses
the otherwise inexplicit, *pragmatic* dimension of the historical documents
themselves. We may define this dimension as the way in which a sacred
text both interprets some salvific moment in the history of an ancient community *and* signifies the possibility of salvific action in the life of the community that reads this history. In *Revelation Restored,* for example,
Halivni reads the biblical story of Ezra as evidence that Ezra, under divine
guidance, restored Israel's Torah after destruction. At the same time, he interprets Ezra's restorative work as figure of the restorative work that the
rabbinic sages performed after the Second Destruction *and that we can
perform, again, after the destructions that define our epoch.* Halivni ad-
dresses his words, in particular, to the perplexed religious Jews of the contemporary academy as well as the perplexed critically minded Jews of the
contemporary yeshiva. He seeks to show both groups how, contrary to
their fears, they can lead pious lives at the same time as they examine with
critical clarity the sacred texts on which their piety rests. Nevertheless, his
pragmatic lesson may apply more generally: that, in the tradition of Ezra,
the judgments that guide postcritical theology must draw on both cognitive
and emotive-spiritual energies, on intimate familiarity with the sacred text
tradition, on a heart enflamed by love of God, of revealed text, and of humanity, and on a profound sense of responsibility to correct blemishes in
the text tradition—as if this tradition constituted the creation itself, as if
that creation were broken, and as if those few with the power to mend the
creation must do so at once.

Foreword:
A Christian Perspective

STANLEY M. HAUERWAS, SERIES COEDITOR

Until recently many Jews and most Christian theologians have accepted as a truism the claim that "Jews do not do theology." To make such a claim is but a way of saying that Jews do not think like Christians. Christians have thought that Jews thinking are rabbis arguing law. Jews have thought that Christians thinking are university theologians engaged in philosophical speculations about the existence of God. These characterizations have been a comforting deceit for Jews and Christians alike, because they have allowed us to "appreciate" one another without assuming that we have anything to do with or to learn from one another.

Yet no Christian can read David Weiss Halivni's *Revelation Restored* without a shock of recognition. This is theology; Jews do theology. Not only is this book theology, but the issues with which Halivni is struggling are also issues that are at the heart of contemporary Christian theological concerns. Without warning, Jews are doing theology in a way that makes it impossible for Christians to ignore.[1] Such a development may make many Christians uncomfortable just to the extent that it now challenges the assumptions inherent in the claim "Jews do not do theology." What has happened that such a challenge, which in truth has always been "there," can now be recognized by Christians?

First, Christians have awakened to their responsibility to respond to the horrors of the Holocaust. Christians know somewhere in the story that makes them Christian that the Shoah that happened to the Jews also continues to have its consequences for Christians. There simply cannot be a truthful account of the convictions that make us Christians that does not make it necessary to tell what happened in that time called Holocaust as part of the Christian story. Christians have only begun to explore how such a telling should work, but we know that such exploration cannot be avoided. The tear the Holocaust made in Christian tradition is no doubt different than that for the Jews, but like the Jews, Christians know that the God we worship makes *tikkun* not only possible but necessary.

Second, Christians have awakened to the disestablishment of their religion as an imperial power. For centuries, Christians have assumed that their worship of a crucified messiah was a formula for rule. Even the loss of a secular political power did not disabuse Christians of such presumption. If it was impossible for us to rule through the office of political power, Christians assumed we would at least continue to rule through "cultural influence." Though such ambitions still possess the souls of most Christians in the West, it is increasingly clear that Christians must learn, like the Jews, to live by learning to read. Skills of survival can only be learned by attending to the witnesses of the past found in Scripture and tradition. We survive by learning to read: the kind of survival skill exemplified by Halivni as he helps Christians see that all reading exhibits as well as requires a politics.[2]

It may be, in this strange time between times, that God is about helping Christians discover how to read our Scriptures in a new way, a way that helps us see how the salvation for the world we believe was wrought in Jesus is not different than what has always been present in Israel. After all, we Christians must learn from Israel how to tell our history as a confession of sin, since we have confidence that it is only from God that we receive redemption from our sins. Does Israel "stumble" (Romans 11)? Yes, the prophets of Israel say so in the "written Torah"; and we learn from Halivni, the rabbis say so in the "oral Torah" recorded in the Talmud: "Had not Israel sinned, only the Pentateuch and the book of Joshua would have been given to them."[3] But, Halivni adds, Ezra restored Israel's Torah and committed Israel to the life of religious law and of studying the oral Torah that repairs Israel's breach. Does the Church stumble? Yes, Paul says so: "I am told that when you meet as a congregation you all fall into sharply divided groups. . . . The result is that when you meet as a congregation, it is impossible for you to eat the Lord's Supper" (1 Cor. 11: 18–20). But through the confession of sin, such stumbling brings also our redemption: "If we examined ourselves we should not thus fall under judgment. When, however, we do fall under the Lord's judgment, he is disciplining us, to save us from being condemned with the rest of the world" (I Cor. 11:31–32). When it tries to forget Israel, the Church tries also to forget its own stumbling and thereby loses its means of redemption. We hope that what is happening through Christian disestablishment is a fresh discovery not only of our sin but also of the continuing witness of God's people, the Jews.

This discovery is made more vivid by our loss of confidence in modernist intellectual formations. "Objectivity," " the text," and other assumed "givens" turn out to be the way that Christians tried to universalize our faith so that Judaism could be left behind. Yet the very means we used for that project hid from us the inescapable timefulness of our faith. As a result, we lost the ability to read our Scriptures in a manner consonant with our conviction that in Jesus God has made us part of God's covenant with Abraham. Accordingly, the words of Scripture matter in the same way that it matters that Israel is God's promised people and that Jesus is very God and very man.[4]

"In the same way," however, names not a result but an ongoing task. It is precisely this task that the series *Radical Traditions* is about. In *Revelation Restored*, Halivni displays the confidence in God and the unapologetic passion for theological work that we hope will characterize all the books in this series. *Radical Traditions* is possible because there now exist authors who share Halivni's passion. Our hope is that through this series their numbers will only increase. Without such hope, a hope that requires that the promised One of Israel be who we learn he is through Torah, this project would be unintelligible. If such a "wager," as Peter Ochs points out in his Foreword, were not required, then we would not be the people of the Book.

Acknowledgments

I would like to express my thanks to Peter Ochs, for recommending this book to the publisher (and for his foreword—as well as to Stanley Hauerwas for his foreword) and above all, for having convinced me that my "transcendent history" will be compatible with contemporary thinking. Also, thanks to Marian Safran of Westview Press for her penetrating and thorough editorial work; no detail escaped her scrupulous eye, and to my student assistant Jonah Steinberg who not only took care of the technical tasks so essential in producing a modern manuscript but also participated in and lived the writing of this book.

David Weiss Halivni

Revelation Restored

Forty days after the giving of the Torah, when the children of Israel danced around the golden calf proclaiming, "This is your God, Israel, who brought you out of Egypt" (Exodus 32:8), revelation was suspended.

Seven hundred years later, when the children of Israel returned from Babylonian captivity, repenting and singling out the sin of having proclaimed the golden calf to be "your God who brought you out of Egypt" (Nehemiah 9:18), revelation was restored.

Introduction

This book explores the editorial policy evident in the canonization of the Hebrew Pentateuch, as well as the various traditions in Jewish law and lore that grew out of the circumstances surrounding this canonization. Yet even as it seeks an understanding of the human agencies necessarily involved in the earliest preservation, arrangement, and interpretation of the Pentateuch, this book presupposes that to speak of such agencies is not necessarily to belie the divinity of the scriptural word. Indeed, this book achieves its unique perspective by investigating a continual relationship between the human stewardship of the scriptures and their divine origin. To a large extent, the project arises from the work that was begun in *Peshat and Derash: Plain and Applied Meaning in Rabbinic Exegesis* and, in particular, from some of the ideas that were raised in the theological segment of that book. Critics have raised important questions requiring clarification, and the following pages will respond to some of these concerns while presenting an approach to the history of the Hebrew canon and its interpretation that should stand on its own as a contribution to modern Jewish thought, academic and theological.

The problem that gave rise to the theology of *Peshat and Derash* will be the central issue of this book, namely, how can it be that the text that resides at the very core of Judaism, the Pentateuch itself, is susceptible to textual criticism that reveals it to be both internally uneven and apparently inconsistent with observed Jewish law? This is both an academic question of religious and literary history and a pressing theological challenge. On the one hand, we must survey the textual record of Jewish history and appraise the ways in which Judaism has dealt with the difficulties posed by its sacred canon. On the other hand, we shall have to respond to the modern religious Jew who confronts the maculation of the written holy word.

The incongruities of the Pentateuch, and its disparities with observed laws, are not the new discoveries of modern textual science. In fact, traditional sources dating back to the time of canonization itself seem already to have struggled with the insufficiency of the Pentateuch's literal surface, searching the text for hidden meanings and mining the tradition for corrective oral law. No learned Jew has ever been oblivious of the canonical scriptures' inability to stand alone. Though the tides of theological dogma concerning the independence of the written word have turned and turned again, as shall be shown, the need for adjunct explication and expansion has always been addressed. The great difference in our time is that modern sensibilities can no longer accept old solutions on faith. No matter how the textual problems were resolved in the classical rabbinic texts, the modern Jew remains troubled by the very need for such solutions. As the rigors of analytical science have occluded the comforts of mythology in the human psyche, the modern religious Jew has become ever more unable to believe that maculation in the scriptural Torah does not exist as such.

We must therefore begin with the premise that the literal surface of the canonical Pentateuch is marred by contradictions, lacunae, and various other maculations whose provenance appears more human than divine. The innovation of this book, in its historical and analytic work, will be to propose that some of the problems that trouble the modern critical scholar were already known to the very people responsible for canonization itself. We shall trace the history of the canonical word from a point of departure at which its purveyors themselves knew it to be imperfect. Pointing out the means by which these agents of canonization worked to make their legacy viable nonetheless, I shall suggest an answer to the question of how they could, in good conscience, have passed on a text whose problems they recognized very well. Moving on through the history of subsequent Judaism, we will study the interplay between the maculate written word and corrective oral traditions or exegesis as this relationship proceeded through several stages, consonant always with the intellectual spirit of the age and leading finally to the theological challenge of the present day—Jewish faith confronted by the science of textual criticism.

Finally, I shall address this theological challenge. The historical survey begins by recognizing that the written Torah is maculate; the theological argument must begin with the selfsame premise. As in its historical analysis, the innovation of this book in its theological argument will be to assume that the textual problems in question were at issue at the time of canonization as well. Beginning with this premise (whose historical plausibility will have been demonstrated by Chapters 1 and 2, the analytical chapters of this book), I shall, in Chapter 3, outline the opportunities for theological advancement that present themselves once it has been concluded that the prophetic sponsors of the sacred word, at the very time of its canonization, were aware of maculations in the text. From the perspective of tradition, this starting point is not so revolutionary as it may seem. In fact, the survey will reveal substantial acknowledgment in traditional Jewish sources of a restorative project at the time of the return from Babylonian captivity. Both evidence within the later books of the Bible, and more-explicit statements in early rabbinic literature, attest to a restorative editorial role for Ezra the Scribe, the religious leader of Israel at the time of the return from exile. Moreover, this evidence in traditional sources indicates that the notion of an editorial project with respect to the Pentateuch was, in fact, theologically acceptable to the rabbis of ages past. Indeed, the concept of Ezra's editorial prerogative was employed by several illustrious rabbinic commentators to account for the literal surface of the Pentateuch, as we shall see.

Consequently, as in *Peshat and Derash*, the role of Ezra, as the biblical prophetic leader presiding at the time of canonization, will be of central importance. Since critics of my previous work have taken issue especially with the role that I ascribe to Ezra, I shall restate my position here, framing the argument that the following pages will support. This clarification will, I hope, dispel some basic misunderstandings of *Peshat and Derash* that evidently have arisen among its critics.

According to the biblical account, it was Ezra who brought forth the Holy Scriptures and presented them to the people of Israel upon the nation's return from captivity in Babylon. It was Ezra who vouched for the written word, ensuring its sacred status with his prophetic endorsement. As the people of Israel repented the sins of the exiled generation and declared their willingness to embrace God's word, it was Ezra who brought this word to the people.

That is not to say that the Torah was revealed by God to Ezra, in effective supervention of the traditional revelation to Moses on Mount Sinai. At least one illustrious rabbinic commentator of the Middle Ages went as far as to claim that it does not matter whether the Torah was revealed through Moses or through Ezra;[1] but even if we speculated that the canonical Torah was revealed anew, word for word, to Ezra, we could not thereby account for persisting maculations in the text. Rather, Ezra's role, seen from the perspective of tradition, must remain secondary to that of Moses, but of central necessity nonetheless. In fact R. Yose, in the Talmud (B.T. Sanhedrin 21b and parallels), states, "Had the Torah not been revealed to Moses, it would have been revealed to Ezra." This proverbial passage deserves our close attention. No other steward of God's word could be so aptly likened to Moses in Jewish tradition as Ezra, and yet the difference between these two figures is crucial as well, as the Talmudic quotation suggests. Ezra was not only the final biblical prophet; he also was the prophet in whose time the people of Israel, at long last, embraced the Torah. Moses, by tradition, was the prophet of original revelation, the medium through which God's will came to his people. But the people of Moses' time, also according to tradition, were unfit and unprepared to hear the word of God. The people "stood at a distance" as the Torah was revealed. Only in Ezra's day did the nation gather around, willing and eager to receive the written word. In this sense, the work of Ezra completes the work of Moses.

The Torah was revealed to Moses, but received, hundreds of years later, under Ezra. Yet the two prophetic figures are not entirely analogous. Whereas Moses must be seen as a passive conduit, the recipient of a perfect, divine Torah, Ezra must be seen as a prophet whose task was to rebuild that Torah. Ascribing this role to Ezra is not only a theological maneuver (that is, not merely a proposition posited in order to uphold faith) but an academic one as well (that is, a plausible historical assertion). Through viewing Ezra's work as a project of restoration, we may explain the various problems of the canonical text.

In *Peshat and Derash,* I introduced a theological position that I entitled *"Chate'u Yisrael"*—translated literally: "Israel sinned." This idea allows the modern religious Jew, appraised of critical responses to the scriptures, to understand how an actual revelation of God's will at Sinai is compatible with a Torah that shows signs of having been compiled from several textual strands. According to the biblical account itself, the people of Israel forsook the Torah, in the dramatic episode of the golden calf, only forty days after the revelation at Sinai. From that point on, until the time of Ezra, the scriptures reveal that the people of Israel were steeped in idolatry and negligent of the Mosaic law. *Chate'u Yisrael,* as a theological account, explains that in the period of neglect and syncretism the Torah of Moses became blemished and maculated. The need to reconstitute and canonize the scriptural Torah in Ezra's time, according to *Chate'u Yisrael,* arose from the textual difficulties caused by centuries of neglect.

The historical and literary analysis of this book will support the modern critical claim that the Torah was assembled from the elements of preexisting tradition; and the theological portion of the book will affirm this conclusion. Scrutiny of the historical record, as well as close reading of traditional exegesis, will help us to understand that the Torah embraced by Israel upon the nation's return from exile was the result of a project of reconstructive compilation. In brief, we shall conclude that Ezra and his entourage of scribes and leaders brought together a text composed of the most authoritative and sacred writings extant in the Israelite tradition of their day. They presented this work to the people and pronounced it to be the record of Sinaitic revelation. *Chate'u Yisrael,* as a theological position, allows us to say that the components brought together in this compilation of the Pentateuch, under the prophetic supervision of Ezra, were the remains of an authentic revelation to Moses in the wilderness—a legacy that had become blemished after centuries of Israelite neglect and idolatry in the preexilic age.

Chate'u Yisrael is a religious idea. It is a conclusion of faith, based on loyalty to the inherited tradition that God broke into human history to reveal his will once and for all. Mosaic revelation cannot be proven or disproved; it resides in the deepest recesses of history and the soul as a national account of origin and meaning. Those who wish to remain within this tradition of faith, while still embracing some benefits of a modern, critical outlook, may choose to join me in the belief that the work of canonization was undertaken on the sacred remnants of a real revelation. This idea is central to the theological argument of this book, and it is compatible with the best possible analysis of the work of canonization.

In the twenty-fifth chapter of his *Guide of the Perplexed,* Maimonides concerned himself with the Aristotelian axiom of the eternity of the universe. Maimonides justified his rejection of the hegemonic Aristotelian view in the following manner:

> Know that our shunning of the affirmation of the eternity of the world is not due to a text figuring in the *Torah* according to which the world has been produced in time. For the texts indicating that the world has been produced in time are not more numerous than those indicating that the deity is a body. Nor are the gates of figurative interpretation shut in our faces or impossible of access to us regarding the subject of the creation of the world in time. For we could interpret them as figurative, as we have done when denying His corporeality. Perhaps this would even be much easier to do. . . .
>
> Two causes are responsible for our not doing this or believing it. One of them is as follows . . . the eternity of the world has not been demonstrated. Consequently in this case the texts ought not to be rejected and figuratively interpreted in order to make prevail an opinion whose contrary can be made to prevail by means of various sorts of arguments. This is one cause.
>
> The second cause is as follows. Our belief that the deity is not a body destroys for us none of the foundations of the Law and does not give lie to the claims of any prophet. The only objection to it is constituted by the fact that the ignorant think that this belief is contrary to the text; yet it is not contrary to it, as we have explained, but is intended by the text. On the other hand, the belief in eternity the way Aristotle sees it—that is, the belief according to which the world exists in virtue of necessity, that no nature changes at all, and that the customary course of events cannot be modified with regard to anything—destroys the Law in its principle, necessarily gives lie to every miracle, and reduces to inanity all the hopes and threats that the Law has held out, unless—by God!—one interprets the miracles figuratively also, as was done by Islamic internalists; this, however, would result in some sort of crazy imaginings.[2]

My position on the revelation at Sinai as the source of the original Torah is analogous to Maimonides' tenacity with respect to the creation of the world in time. In the first place, no one critical theory of the Pentateuch's origins has been proven. Almost all the data are disputed among the various factions of scientific scholars. Consequently, I see no cause to reject the notion of a Torah from Heaven. We shall not undermine centuries of faith on the basis of critical theories whose contraries can be made to prevail by means of various sorts of arguments.

In the second place, the course that we shall take in examining the scriptures destroys none of the foundations of the Torah and does not give lie to the claims of any prophet. We shall not upset any of the basic and essential tenets of Jewish faith. These tenets, however, would be upset if we were to abandon the traditional view of a definitive revelation at Sinai. Belief in the divine origin of the Law is the crux of Jewish religion, tenaciously preserved throughout the ages, guaranteeing the preservation of Judaism itself. Critical approaches that eradicate the notion of divine revelation destroy the Law in its principle, necessarily give lie to every miracle, and reduce to inanity all the hopes and threats that the Law has held out—not to mention all the joys and the trials, the accomplishments and the martyrdoms, that have attended Jewish fealty to the Law throughout the ages.

Like Maimonides in his day, I am unwilling to disturb the foundation of Judaism on so basic a level by rushing to become allied with theories that cannot be proven. The scholarly debates concerning the formation of the various textual traditions identified within the Pentateuch are fierce and unresolved and therefore not theologically compelling. Critical scholars who straddle the fence of tradition and who are convinced that modern findings do belie the lore of Moses have already begun to develop theological positions that account for the Torah in the absence of a revelation at Sinai. I do not feel that such radical steps are necessary or beneficial. The Torah still, for me, remains aloof, above these speculations. The belief in a divine event at Sinai is the creedal foundation of religious Judaism. Know that the gates of figurative interpretation are not closed to us. Yet we see no need to challenge the Law at its very foundations when its problematic features may yet be accounted for without recourse to the denial of Sinai.

In the chapters to follow, we shall see how the literary evidence of the Bible itself, and of the earliest extrascriptural traditions, demonstrates that the agents of canonization were aware of maculations in their holy text. Remarkably, however, we shall conclude that Ezra and his entourage, despite their prophetic stature and their intimacy with the written word, were unable to impose corrective alterations on the text itself. Even as they confronted the need to supplement the written word with adjunct explication, the agents of canonization treated their scriptural legacy as a sacred and inviolable trust. Although the resolution of difficulties emanating from the text was immediately necessary, the scriptural word was not susceptible to alteration, even by those who compiled the holy canon in the period of return from exile. There is ample evidence in the later books of the Bible and in the earliest oral law to substantiate the following two important facts: first, that the literal surface of the canonical Pentateuch was problematic even to its earliest proponents; and second, that, nonetheless, this scriptural word was inviolable. In the pages to follow we shall investigate the special need of Ezra and his entourage to hold their text above reproof while at the same time dealing with its maculations. In brief, this inviolability of the scriptures to their canonizers is itself the strongest evidence that the texts compiled into the current Torah were regarded by the scribes themselves as the legacy of a true and early revelation.

The notion arising from polemics of the Middle Ages that God, the perfect being, could not have created an imperfect instrument, subject to human corruption, strikes me as totally unfounded.[3] The divinity of the scriptural word is not diminished by human error. One does not have to deny that God created the world because of the mess that humankind has enacted in it. In fact, it would be surprising if the situation with regard to the written Torah were otherwise—if, among all the things that humankind has blemished, only the written record of the divine word has remained immune.

Even if *Chate'u Yisrael* as a basis for religious faith is accepted by the modern religious Jew, a central theological problem remains with respect to the written Torah. If we must recognize that the written Torah is a compiled text, encoding the problematic consequences of a difficult history of transmission, how can we still revere this Torah as divine writ? The theological argument of this book will be that revelation did occur, and that the canonical Torah, the troubled textual remnant of this divine event, was corrigible by means of oral law. But that still leaves us with the maculated text itself. The religious Jew kisses this text as it is carried in procession about the synagogue. How can that Jew continue to do so while acknowledging the problems of the Torah's past?

This is the point at which the prophetic role of Ezra enters the theological argument of this book. I shall speak of the restorative role of Ezra in supplementing maculated written laws with explanatory oral ones; but I must also address his legacy of text—the canonical written Pentateuch.

First a serious misunderstanding that has marked the major criticisms of *Peshat and Derash* must be dispelled. The theological argument of *Chate'u Yisrael* also posits that written laws that had become corrupt in the course of Israelite neglect and idolatry were restored to their original intentions by means of oral law. Somehow, for example, the written text of the Pentateuch came to demand "an eye for an eye," and yet the earliest oral traditions substitute pecuniary compensation. *Chate'u Yisrael* allows us to conclude that oral law, as a legacy transmitted along with the written Torah, actually restored the biblical commandment to its original state.

Critics have assumed that *Chate'u Yisrael* represents a "maximalistic" position with respect to the Sinaitic origins of rabbinic oral law. Some have suggested that, having revealed the human and time-bound factors involved in Jewish commentary and exegesis throughout the ages, I then discard these insights in the theological portion of *Peshat and Derash* and espouse the extreme view that each and every rabbinic explication of the written word restores the Pentateuchal text to its original literal appearance at Sinai. That was not the aim of the argument. *Peshat and Derash* was not meant to claim that every minute point of rabbinic lore is a restorative agent of the kind just explained. Rather, *Peshat and Derash* dealt with the cases in which oral tradition displaced the literal meaning of the written word entirely—and those are relatively few. In the special cases in which oral law is absolutely inconsonant with the scriptural text (such as the case of *lex talionis,* where pecuniary compensation is required instead of physical compensation), the doctrine of *Chate'u Yisrael* proposes restorative action as an explanation. There are numerous other instances in which the oral tradition mandates observances that are not immediately apparent from a reading of the scriptural Pentateuch. Inasmuch as these laws do not actually contradict the written word, they belong to a different category and deserve theological attention of a different sort. Again, we are here concerned with instances in which the oral law is incompatible, unequivocally, with the written word.

In fact, the restorative action credited to oral law in *Peshat and Derash* was not meant to be understood as arising from the rabbis themselves. As we shall see, textual evidence indicates that almost all of the instances in which religious practice divergent from the scriptural word was required were already taken for granted by the time of the earliest rabbinic writings. The laws of levirate marriage, as they are still mandated in rabbinic law, for example, were well established by the time of the rabbis, although these laws involve an effective emendation of the scriptural text, as we shall see.

My thesis is that the religious mind does not willfully depart from the holy word for any reason. The very fact that there are instances in which religious law diverges from the scriptures indicates that some factor must have mitigated the sacred status of the text at these loci, allowing the literal meaning to be displaced. If at some point in history the religious authorities of Judaism felt that the practical import of the holy text ought to be altered, they must have had strong grounds to suspect the written record of being maculate. One cannot assume that a devout religious mind would tolerate drifting departures from the divine word. I propose instead that such departures were mandated, with great care, in special instances in which the holy text was known to be problematic.

If certain scholarly opinions are correct, then such careful departures from the written text may be compared to the well-known system of *keri* and *ketiv*. In this system, certain scriptural words, when read aloud, are given pronunciations that depart from their canonical orthography. The alternate readings (correct readings, according to this tradition) are preserved as an adjunct tradition to the biblical canon, whereas the written word itself is preserved unchanged. No religious Jew would suggest that the scroll of the Torah be altered to reflect the *keri* (the pronunciations when the pertinent words are read aloud), and yet the *ketiv* (those written words themselves) is considered invalid if pronounced in a ritual reading according to their actual orthography. According to one traditional view, *keri* and *ketiv* arise from doubts concerning the correct text, doubts that resulted from the years of Babylonian exile. According to this view, by the time the Jews returned from Babylon, some of their written text had diverged from the known pronunciations and yet the people were not certain enough of the errors, or of the correct text, to effect the appropriate emendations.

Although the exile is a possible explanation for some textual problems, I cannot accept this theory in accounting for all the difficulties of the written word. For one thing, the period of exile was simply too short to have generated a need for the comprehensive reconstruction that evidently took place in the time of Ezra. I prefer to suggest that the maculations of the text, great and small, are the consequence of a more terrible and protracted period of corruption—ages of idolatry and syncretism in the period of Israelite settlement in the Land and in the period of the First Temple.

Whatever the cause of textual maculation, one must conclude that with respect to those places where rabbinic law departs irreconcilably from the written word, religious loyalty to this written word cannot have been complete. Some other factor must have entered on the scene. The *Chate'u Yisrael* theory proposes that the other agent was a restorative knowledge of original divine intent, passed through the generations, most likely by a very small and loyal minority, even as the written text became corrupt. Those who disagree might suggest that behavior resulting from popular tendencies or socioeconomic concerns pushed the written text aside. Scholars have indeed suggested that rabbinic law gave in to popular practice and socioeconomic realities, mitigating the written word in accordance with opinion and sentiment at large. I cannot find that explanation satisfying. It is extremely difficult to imagine that a religious rabbinic mind of any age would knowingly allow a holy law to be washed away on a tide of popular opinion. Knowing how much the rabbis resisted public opinion on minor issues, or nonissues (such as customs), it is difficult to imagine that they would have yielded to popular opinion on such a major issue as a biblical law, phrase, or word. Nor can socioeconomic factors be held responsible for deviations from the written word. Some far more authoritative factor must account for the changes.

Nevertheless, even if we accept the idea that departures from the written word were undertaken on the basis of original divine intent, we must return to the sacred status of the written word itself. How can a text be holy when it is not followed? Here we must appreciate the legacy of Ezra. The contrite and zealous returnees from Babylonian captivity—the nascent Jewish people—required laws by which to reforge their land and covenant. The religious leadership, under Ezra, apparently was able to satisfy this need, instructing the people on the details of observance. At the same time, the people needed a sign to elevate as evidence of the Mosaic covenant; and in this capacity the written Torah emerged. In Ezra's estimation, the written Torah, problematic as it was, constituted the best compiling of the scattered shards of revelation, and Ezra was a prophet. Therefore, the maculate Torah was elevated to a holy ritual status beyond correction, even as corrective traditions were introduced through adjunct oral law.

The religious Jew may trust Ezra in good faith. In apparent paradox, the written Torah, if followed to the literal word, may not be valid in religious law. Yet as a symbol of the covenant, it has the highest possible endorsement—the stamp of prophetic approval. This theological idea—a supplement to *Chate'u Yisrael*—will be explored in great detail in Chapter 3, the theological chapter of this book.

I should add that throughout this book, the word "history" refers to more than factual events as best as they may be established from such evidence as the books of Ezra and Nehemiah, assuming that these records present more than an idealized narrative. "History" is also used here to include the impression that the recorded events project and generate in the perceiver's mind. That might best be called "transcendent history," since what the historian perceives is more than the sum total of the events recorded. The reader of a historical record perceives its data in a setting that transcends the mere facts themselves and that allows events to be placed in a meaningful, sequential, evolutionary pattern. To catalog events without taking into account the effect they have upon the consciousness of the perceiver is tantamount to conveying only partial information. Elsewhere I have remarked:

> One does not have to be especially creative or particularly imaginative to understand a text when one has read one. Such intellectual activity does not complement reality. It merely focusses on it. But one cannot understand the full significance of a text without transcending it, without reaching into its evolutionary past. That only an intuitive grasp can yield such an understanding does not diminish its veracity. A text, like a human being, is true to itself only when it is more than itself. [4]

1

The Compilers' Editorial Policy

Traditional and Critical Perspectives

The religious scholar within the Jewish tradition takes it for granted that the book of Deuteronomy is the final chapter of the Pentateuch. The weight of tradition and the narrative of Deuteronomy itself have firmly established this book as the last segment in the Torah of Moses, representing the last words of the Prophet to his people in the wilderness. Most of those within the fold regard alternative chronologies as suspect in the extreme. Yet since the advent of that scholarship known as Higher Biblical Criticism, a debate has raged in the academy concerning the chronological relationship of "P," the priestly code and textual tradition associated with the book of Leviticus, and "D," the Deuteronomic scriptures. In fact, until recently, the favored arguments in this dispute have ascribed later authorship to "P," making the priests of Jerusalem the final contributors to the Pentateuch, perhaps even accomplishing their work in the Babylonian exile of the sixth century B.C.E. Prominent theories of religious evolution, stressing the antecedence of narrative and miracle to law and ritual detail, have been called upon to ratify the claim that the intricate Levitical code represents the latest developments in the religion of biblical Israel.

Most recently, however, especially among a new generation of Israeli and Jewish critical scholars,[1] the traditional place of Deuteronomy as the last of the Pentateuch's books has regained scholarly acceptance, albeit for reasons grounded in critical theory. As evidence for Deuteronomy's late arrival, scholars point to the Jerusalem-based centrality of worship dominant in the Deuteronomic outlook, ascribing this phenomenon to a period in which the priesthood of Jerusalem was well established.

Neither side of this academic dispute has entirely vindicated itself. Without recourse to tradition, one can argue either way. In this book, I will not make claims of precedence for one textual element or another. The evidence of critical scholarship does not compel one to abandon the belief that the Pentateuch has its origins at Sinai. Therefore, we shall proceed from a later point in biblical history and from a conclusion that has been accepted by traditional and critical scholars alike. This point of departure is the accepted fact that the people of Israel, upon their return from captivity in Babylon in the sixth century B.C.E., embraced a scriptural Pentateuch in which all of the textual elements identified in the current scholarly debate had been consolidated.[2]

The Return from Babylonian Captivity

The biblical narrative describes the period of return from exile (following the conquest of the Babylonian empire by the Persian Cyrus in 539 B.C.E.) as a time of national and religious rebirth. According to the biblical accounts in the books of Ezra and Nehemiah, the return from exile was characterized in particular by two religious phenomena. In the first place, the returning Israelites collectively expressed repentance for the ages of idolatry and syncretism, which they saw as the cause of their ancestors' expulsion from the Land. At the same time, the people expressed a zeal to embrace the Law of their God, the Torah of Moses, from Mount Sinai. Historians of biblical Israel concur that this period of return saw an unprecedented desire, in the renascent land, for scriptural religious law. Critical scholars of the Bible believe that this is the time in which the Five Books of Moses were arranged in their present form, the time of the Pentateuch's canonization.

The notion of a "canonization" at any time subsequent to Sinai may initially appear disagreeable, even intolerable, from the traditional point of view. To speak of there having been "editorial policy" in Ezra's day may seem to contravert the legacy of revelation. Therefore, it should be stressed at the outset that this "critical" perspective, which suggests a project of textual standardization in the time of return from exile, may draw support, not only from vague and disputable echoes of this project within the Pentateuch itself, but also from more explicit indications preserved in the later books of the Bible and in the earliest rabbinic traditions. As we begin this investigation, we may find theological encouragement in the fact that the notion of an "editorial" project in the time of Ezra was evidently not unpalatable to some of the earliest rabbis. In the course of this chapter, we shall encounter rabbinic opinions that ascribe to Ezra the role of editor, indicating that choices concerning the form and content of the canonical Pentateuch were made at the time of the return from exile. At the same time, we shall also see that the memory of this canonization has been almost entirely obscured throughout the subsequent centuries of Jewish commentary.

A Change of Heart

First of all, we must touch briefly upon the biblical evidence that documents Israel's zeal to embrace the scriptural Torah in the period of return from exile. The prophetic books that predate Babylonian captivity uniformly address Israel as a backsliding nation, exhorting the people to forsake their wayward behavior and return to the Torah and God. Indeed, from the moment of revelation on Sinai itself, according to the traditional account, the Mosaic law and its champions—the judges, the prophets, and the priests—were obliged to wage a tireless and rarely successful struggle against the idolatrous tendencies of the nation. The episode of the golden calf, under the very clouds of Mount Sinai itself, is a dramatic illustration of Israel's lack of religious resolve. Time and time again, the prophets take God's part in a struggle between heritage and idolatry. The fine details of ritual and law are rarely the subject of these exhortations. Rather, the most basic concepts of fealty to tradition and the most general matters of observance are at issue in these "disputes" between God and his people, mediated through the prophets. The prophets lament Israel's inability to remember its God and to observe his most fundamental precepts, and in essence, they do not demand much more. As long as the heart of the nation is averted from its God, the details of the Torah are not merely beyond the realistic expectation of the prophets. Observing these details would be a travesty without the right intentions. Nonobservance would be preferable to observing the Sabbath punctiliously in honor of Baal or Kemosh. One may go as far as to say that as long as the people of Israel were idol worshippers, they were better off not observing the law. To have observed the laws of Sinai, but not in exclusive allegiance to the God of Abraham, Isaac, and Jacob, would have been more sinful than neglect itself. The prophets of preexilic times did well to exhort the people to the most basic faith and covenantal fealty, leaving the more specific requirements for a later and more faithful age. Not that such details of the covenant were unknown to the prophets; they were known, but there was no sense in urging the nation to fulfill them so long as the observances might have been twisted to deepen the prevalent commitment to syncretistic idolatry.

The books that narrate and follow the return from exile tell of an extraordinary change of heart. The return to the Land itself is recounted in the Bible in terms of the nation's enthusiasm to restore a covenant with the God of its ancestors. The returnees themselves are not merely eager to embrace the concept of a Torah from Sinai; they are equally zealous to translate its details into practice. The scriptural Torah itself, as an actual scroll, is presented dramatically in the biblical narrative at this point, and the people seem eager to make it their own. Where once it was the lonely and beleaguered domain of the prophets and the priests, the Torah of Moses, in the account of the return from Babylonian captivity, appears in popular demand—sought after by the people of Israel at large. The book of Nehemiah provides dramatic testimony. I shall quote the text at length so that the reader may envision the events as they are vividly described, and also because this citation, in its details, supports my frequent references to Ezra's "entourage" as the group that facilitated the people's embrace of the canon.

> When the seventh month came—the people of Israel being settled in their towns—all the people gathered together into the square before the Water Gate. They told the scribe Ezra to bring the book of the Law of Moses which the lord had given to Israel. Accordingly, the priest Ezra brought the Law before the assembly, both men and women and all who could hear with understanding. This was on the first day of the seventh month. He read from it facing the square before the Water Gate from early morning until midday, in the presence of the men and the women and those who could understand; and the ears of the people were attentive to the book of the Law. The scribe Ezra stood on a wooden platform that had been made for the purpose; and beside him stood Mittithiah, Shema, Anaiah, Uriah, Hilkiah and Maaseiah on his right hand and Pedaiah, Mishael, Malchijah, Hashum, Hash-baddanah Zechariah and Meshullam on his left hand. And Ezra opened the book in the sight of all the people, for he was standing above all the people; and when he opened it, all the people stood up. Then Ezra blessed the Lord, the great God, and all the people answered, "Amen, Amen," lifting up their hands. Then they bowed their heads and worshiped the Lord with their faces to the ground. Also Jeshua, Bani, Sherebiah, Jamin, Akkub, Shabbethai, Hodiah, Maaseiah, Kelita, Azariah, Jozaban, Hanan, Pelaiah, the Levites helped the people to understand the Law while the people remained in their places. So they read from the book of the Law of God, with interpretation. They gave the sense, so that the people understood the reading. (Neh. 8:1–8)

The book of Nehemiah exemplifies the spirit and the vision of the post-exilic age. Exile in Babylon had entered the collective consciousness of Israel as the disastrous consequence of idolatry and syncretism. The success of the return to Jerusalem was acknowledged to depend upon Israel's separating itself from the nations and their idolatry as the one people distinguished by its unique Torah. At this moment in the biblical account, perhaps even more than at Sinai, the people of Israel became the Nation of the Book. Again, Nehemiah sets the scene:

> Then those of Israelite descent separated themselves from all foreigners, and stood and confessed their sins and the iniquities of their fathers. They stood

up in their place and read from the Book of the Law of the Lord their God for a fourth part of the day, and for another fourth part they made confession and worshiped the Lord their God. (Neh. 9:1–3–Neh. 9: 2–3.)

The Role of Ezra

In the account of Nehemiah, it was Ezra who brought the Torah to the people, and it was Ezra and his entourage who made the scriptures accessible to the nation with public reading and interpretation. The role of Ezra in furnishing Israel with its scriptures has been overlooked to a large extent,[3] not only by critical scholarship, but also by the mainstream of Jewish religious thought. As we shall see in the pages to follow, centuries of exegesis and interpretation have led to a collective vision of history in religious Judaism of the Torah of Moses having been handed down from Sinai to the present day absolutely unchanged. For many religious Jews today, the Torah that is lifted up in the modern synagogue is the selfsame Torah that was handed to Moses on the mountain, both in appearance and in content. Moreover, according to rabbinic tradition, even the "crowns," or ornaments, on the letters of the text are legitimate territory for legal exegesis.[4] Jewish legend has it that God himself filled his time before creation attaching these "crowns" to the letters of the scriptures (B.T. Menahot 29b). Nevertheless, the editorial role of Ezra has not completely vanished from traditional Jewish sources.

A far less often cited passage, in the Talmudic tractate Sanhedrin (B.T. Sanhedrin 21b), raises the issue of Ezra's involvement in shaping the canonical Torah. The fascinating text there reads:

Mar Zutra, or as some say, Mar 'Ukba, said: Originally the Torah was given to Israel in Hebrew characters and in the sacred [Hebrew] language; later, in the times of Ezra, the Torah was given in Ashurith [Assyrian] script and Aramaic language. [Finally], they selected for Israel the Ashurith script and Hebrew language.

It has been taught: R. Yose said: Had Moses not preceded him, Ezra would have been worthy of receiving the Torah for Israel. Of Moses it is written, "And Moses went up to God" (Exod. 19:3), and of Ezra it is written, "He, Ezra, went up from Babylon" (Ezra 7:6). As the going up of the former refers to the [receiving of the] Law, so does the going up of the latter. . . . And even though the Torah was not given through him [Ezra], its writing was changed through him. . . .

It has been taught: Rabbi said: The Torah was originally given to Israel in this [Ashurith] writing. When they [Israel] sinned, it was changed into Ro'atz. But when they repented, [Assyrian characters] were re-introduced. . . .

R. Simeon b. Elazar said on the authority of R. Eliezer b. Parta who spoke on the authority of R. Eleazar of Modi'im: This writing [of the law] was never changed.

At issue in this Talmudic sequence of perspectives is Ezra's involvement in the form of the canonical Pentateuch. At this point, it is sufficient and essential to note that the idea of Ezra's involvement in the presentation of the Torah appeared in the Talmud as a rabbinic position. We also cannot help but notice that this involvement was an issue of dispute in the passages above. Yet even this difference of rabbinic opinion strengthens the probability that Ezra's editorial role was more than a matter of legend and fancy. It is difficult to imagine why anyone would have thought to ascribe an editorial project to Ezra's day had there not actually been such an undertaking. Some memory of a consolidation of the Pentateuch in the return from exile must account for this issue's appearance in the Talmud.

True, the Talmud attributes a plethora of ordinances to a variety of biblical dignitaries, including Ezra. Such attributions are retroactive projections into traditional history, deemed by their authors as befitting the personages they involve—what the authors felt the biblical figures might have, or should have, done or what the authors felt should be done themselves. Even so, it is unlikely that R. Yose, for example, would have attributed to Ezra such basic editorial actions—which, from the point of view of R. Yose's time, must have bordered on blasphemy—without lingering memories of such a reality. Some residual knowledge of the Pentateuch's history would account for the attribution of editorial work to Ezra. Nobody would have attributed a change of scriptural orthography to Ezra without some basis in history, nebulous as that basis might have been. R. Yose and Rabbi would not have concocted this account on their own without some convincing precedent. Moreover, we should note that the Samaritans, too, have a tradition that Ezra had a hand in the consolidation of the scriptures.[5]

Nevertheless, the concept of editorial prerogative in Ezra's time was clearly unpalatable to the last position in the Talmudic sequence cited above (that of R. Simeon b. Eliezer); and that is understandable. The suggestion that any person after Moses—even another prophet—was somehow involved in a matter as fundamental as the language and orthography of the scriptures is a challenging theological proposition. From the position of orthodoxy in any age, such a view threatens to compromise the sanctity of the written word. We may be encouraged by R. Yose's tolerance toward the concept of Ezra's editorial role; but, as we shall discover, the notion that the canonical Pentateuch was subject to an editorial policy of any sort has been almost thoroughly suppressed throughout rabbinic history, the quoted passage in Sanhedrin being one of a very few notable, and valuable, exceptions.[6]

We shall see that Ezra's role in the canonization of the Pentateuch was not confined to presentation and orthography alone, but apparently included attempts to address the problems of the text. In the pages to follow, we shall touch upon the issue of the ten so-called *puncta extraordinaria* in the text of the Pentateuch. Briefly, in ten places in the scroll of the Torah, there appear scribal markings (dots above the line) that seem to indicate that the words and phrases to which they are attached are not to be understood according to their plain meanings. In fact, these markings seem to demarcate spurious or inappropriate words in the scriptural text. Tradition ascribes the introduction of these markings to Ezra; and a passage in Bamidbar Rabbah (3, 13) concerning the ten points ends with this remarkable addendum:

> Some give another reason why the dots are inserted. Ezra reasoned thus: If Elijah [some read "Moses"] comes and asks, "Why have you written these words?" [i.e., Why have you included these suspect passages?], I shall answer, "That is why I dotted these passages." And if he says to me, "You have done well in having written them," I shall erase the dots above them.

Note that this passage from Bamidbar Rabbah does not merely impute the introduction of the *puncta extraordinaria* to Ezra. Far more astonishingly, this segment of rabbinic lore attributes to Ezra the decision to write (or not to write) sentences in the Pentateuchal text!

These implications have not been lost on subsequent rabbinic commentators. Indeed the sixteenth-century scholar Azariah de Rossi (1513–1578) concluded that this text must have been written by a deviant student without his teacher's knowledge.[7] More recently, Rabbi Moshe Feinstein was even more unequivocal in his declaration that this rabbinic passage represented the most unadulterated heresy in its attribution to Ezra of such excessive leeway with the text of the Torah. Thus, he concluded, it must certainly be excised.[8] Rabbi Feinstein's view (which, incidentally, does not account for the parallel occurrences of this passage) is a recent and paradigmatic example of the tendency, throughout rabbinic history, to reject the memories of an actual project of canonization in Ezra's day. This suppression, rather than being the result of manipulative misrepresentation, demonstrates that traditional thought about the Torah has become incompatible with the notion of any human editorial agency.

Still, there have been notable exceptions to this tendency. Rabbi Y. F. Lisser, the author of the *Binyan Yehoshua,* the standard commentary to the *Avot deRabbi Natan,*[9] took no exception to the authenticity of Ezra's editorial role. Instead, commenting on the passage quoted above (as it appeared in *Avot deRabbi Natan*), he wrote, "Ezra ha-Sofer tikken ha-Torah be-tikkun Soferim kefi ha-tzorekh" (Ezra the Scribe corrected the Torah, in the manner of scribal correction, as needed).

In *Peshat and Derash*,[10] I reviewed further rabbinic opinions that support the concept of Ezra's editorial role. Let me here merely reiterate that both Ibn Ezra and Rabbi Jehudah ha-Chasid designated some words, and even phrases, as having been added to the scriptures after the time of Moses.[11] Some of these, according to Jehudah ha-Chasid, were added in the period of the High Synod, Ezra's entourage. The additions could not have been ascribed to a later time, for that would have excluded them from the scriptural time frame and deprived them of authentic biblical sanctity. Still other words and phrases have been identified as the additions (or omissions) of Joshua and David. In the latter cases some connection is drawn between the content of the passages and these personages, whereas in the instances attributed to the High Synod, no such links are made, strengthening the contention that Ezra's entourage was credited with a comprehensive editorial task. In short, even as the concept of an unaltered Torah from Sinai ascended to hegemony, some exceptional rabbinic commentators found Ezra's editorial role indispensable to comprehensive interpretation and theology. The medieval scholar Moses Alshakar went as far as to state, "It makes no difference whether the Torah was given via Moses or via Ezra in terms of whether Sages can exposit upon it."[12] Still, Alshakar's perspective can best be understood in the context of Rabbi's view, in Sanhedrin, that the canonization of the postexilic age was, in fact, a restoration.

Taken at face value, the passage from Bamidbar Rabbah quoted above, with its hypothetical exchange between Ezra and Elijah (or Moses), seems to aim at portraying the concerns of a conscientious editor, entrusted with a precious textual legacy and an enormous religious responsibility. This passage provides traditional corroboration of the "critical" perspective that sees the extant Pentateuch as having undergone a process of compilation and edition in the time of the return from exile. And again, it must be stressed that the insertion of Ezra as an intermediary after Moses would be extremely improbable in the realm of tradition were it not based on historical reality. Moreover, we must recognize that there have been times and circles in rabbinic history in which the notion of Ezra's editorial role was not theologically intolerable.

Ezra's Restoration

The allusions of the postexilic books of the Bible to the content of the Book of the Law, as presented by Ezra, provide good indications that all the various strata identified by critical scholarship as separate textual traditions were included in the canon at that time.[13] The ritual centrality of Jerusalem, for example, ascribed by criticism to the Deuteronomic tradition, and the concern for ritual detail, which is generally identified with Leviticus, appear as an integrated whole in the religious life of Israel after the exile, as narrated in the books of Ezra, Nehemiah, and the Chronicles. Whatever their textual history, the various strands and textual elements identified by critical scholarship had been compiled fully in a canonical Pentateuch at the time of the return from exile. Some critical scholars regard this compilation as the emergence of a Pentateuch for the first time and dispense with the Mosaic revelation at Sinai, even though belief in the revelation runs through the entire Bible and constitutes, as it were, its nervous system. Such academicians consign the entire concept of Mosaic revelation to the realm of mythology, declaring it to be a retrojection by later generations. The evidence, however, does not warrant such a radical departure from tradition. It is quite plausible, by following a path analogous to Rabbi's in the passage from Sanhedrin quoted above, to regard the work of Ezra's day as an endeavor of *restoration,* undertaken on a once-whole Torah that had become maculate. This position accords with the traditional account of Israel's lapse into idolatry immediately following the Torah's revelation, the episode of the golden calf, and the history of idolatry and neglect of covenant imputed to Israel throughout the biblical narrative. Nor is this view only a theological assuagement; in fact, it allows us to account for some of the most persistent problems that surround the canonical text of the Pentateuch. Though it may at first appear a paradox, regarding Ezra's activity as a project that he himself saw as a restoration of a preexisting holy text enables us to account for the existence of persistent maculations in the canonical scriptures.

Before we enter into the details of inconsistencies and analogies, I shall make a general observation concerning the commitment of the people to halakha after the time of Ezra. (It must be noted that we use "halakha" here in a generic sense to mean detailed, scripturally based religious law akin to current Jewish law in much of its substance, and in the premise that observance of the law itself is a means to becoming closer to God, but obviously not identical in extent or in every detail to the halakha of our own day, which is the cumulative product of Jewish piety since Ezra's time.) The perceptive reader will notice that throughout this chapter I have assumed that after Ezra, the people were committed to a system of religious law and lived accordingly. That sets them apart from the masses of Jews during the First Temple period who, because of idolatry, ignored the halakha.

My assumption is contrary to the rapidly ascending opinion among contemporary scholars that the masses during the Second Temple period were either sectarians or Hellenists, with little interest in what later became rabbinic midrash and halakha. Those who were interested, according to this view, were a minority, an elite, as were the monotheistic followers of the Law in the First Temple period. This opinion is common among scholars of Hellenistic and sectarian literature, who tend to see the protagonists of the literature they study as the dominant force of the period. Talmudic and rabbinic scholars, especially those who feel competent enough to utilize relatively later sources for the projection of antecedents, see things differently. To such scholars it is apparent that from soon after Ezra, a sizable, active community existed continuously, and that its tradition found its religious fulfillment centuries later in rabbinic halakha. J. Bright's conclusion, not so long ago, is still worth heeding:

> Through the obscurity of the fourth and third centuries [B.C.E.], development continued along the lines laid down [by Ezra and Nehemiah] until, by the time of the Maccabean Revolt, Judaism, though still in the process of evolvement, had assumed in all essentials the shape characteristic of it in the centuries to come.[14]

Recent revelations from the Dead Sea Scrolls add weight to Bright's analysis. With each publication from the finds in the Judean Desert, the parameters of halakhic behavior are pushed back in time. That was reaffirmed with particular strength by the recent publication of a text from among the Dead Sea Scrolls, known as *Miksat Maase Hatorah (MMT)*. The "oldest" manuscript of this scroll has been determined, through paleographic analysis, to date from around 75 B.C.E. However, studies of the text of *MMT* have concluded that the scroll had been copied over several generations prior to the writing of this particular document, and "there likely existed even older manuscripts which have not survived," reaching back to the second century B.C.E., if not earlier.[15] *MMT* has been evaluated as a polemical summary of the ritual and legal matters in which the Qumran sect differed from its Jerusalem-based adversaries. Unlike the Temple Scroll, for instance, to which it bears striking similarity, *MMT* contains only those laws that were disputed by other sects. We may assume that for any law quoted in the text, there were those who disagreed and held contrary opinions. This assumption is strengthened by the frequent use in the text of the expression "we are of the opinion." Thus, when *MMT* (4Q396. 1–2) says, concerning the ritual slaughter of animals, "We are of the opinion that the fetus found in its slaughtered mother's womb may be eaten only after it (the fetus) has been ritually slaughtered," we are informed that there was a contrary view, held by others, that the fetus, even though alive, was considered ritually dead by virtue of the mother's having been slaughtered. According to the latter position, the ritual slaughter of the mother animal rendered the fetus permissible for eating, as though it were a limb of the mother. Remarkably, the very same controversy was recorded in the Mishnah (Chulin 4:5) in a dispute between R. Meir and the Sages.[16]

I choose this example because of its multiple implications and will mention here only the two most important ones: First, this evidence contradicts the loud voices in recent scholarship that doubt the authenticity and early provenance of classical rabbinic dicta, claiming that such dicta were invented by later editors and imputed to earlier rabbis. Here we have a controversy that the Mishnah recorded in the name of a Tanna of the second century C.E. (R. Meir), and we find that the particulars of this dispute in fact predate this Sage by at least four hundred years. (In a similar development, Yigael Yadin's discovery, in the Judean Desert, of two kinds of phylacteries, dating from the time of the Bar Kochba revolt,[17] caused scholars to reevaluate the famous dispute on the order of parchments within phylacteries—a controversy whose practical consequences had previously been thought to originate with the two famous medieval disputants on the issue, Rashi and Rabbenu Tam.)

Second—and of more import for the discussion here—if, in the second century B.C.E. or earlier,[18] someone was of the opinion that a living animal (called in later Rabbinics a *ben pekuah*) could be considered ritually dead, and could be eaten without being separately slaughtered because the ritual slaughtering of the mother extended also to the fetus and rendered such eating permissible, then the laws of ritual slaughter must have been well entrenched, and particular details and possible hypothetical cases resolved, before this extraordinary case of *ben pekuah* was debated in a sectarian controversy. Moreover, the view that an animal conspicuously alive may yet be considered dead by dint of ritual technicalities represents a legalistic mentality usually associated with the rabbis of the Talmud and attests to a highly developed sense of law at a much earlier time, which can only have flourished in the context of a kind of piety that is best called halakhic. Thus the thesis that soon after the time of Ezra, Jewish commitment generally found its religious fulfillment and expression in halakha is strengthened.[19]

Finally, let me add that throughout this inquiry I have tacitly assumed that soon after the different, indeed contradictory, strands were woven into one text, canonized—which, in the case of the Pentateuch, according to a consensus of scholarly opinion and even according to the critics, took place after the return from Babylonian exile.[20] The Pentateuch became binding to its adherents, and they did not dare to alter the text as long as their adherence continued. Those who broke away and formed their own sect, or quit altogether, naturally differed, partially or more substantially, with the text, accusing the original group of falsification. For those who remained within, however, only imperceptible, gradual, evolutionary changes took place, as reflected in varied readings retained within the group; but the text as a whole remained intact.

This assumption too is probably unacceptable to many scholars. Some believe that canonization of a binding and unalterable Pentateuch did not take place until the late Tannaitic period. Prior to that, the text was not stable and was free to be altered by any justification. The rabbis, such scholarship argues, altered the text—certainly the meaning of the text— whenever they explained it not according to *peshat*. These scholars also point to the Dead Sea Scrolls (and to the Book of Jubilees) as proof of the fluidity of the biblical text, including the Pentateuch. With each discovery of a new manuscript at Qumran, the certainty of a single text is eroded. Each scroll seems to have its own scriptural text, different from one another, and collectively different from our Masoretic text.

However, I do not believe that the Dead Sea Scrolls (or the Book of Jubilees[21]) prove that there was no canonization until centuries after Ezra, well into the rabbinic period. What these scholars seem to confuse is the difference between the collective groups represented by the manuscripts at Qumran not having a single text, and each individual community's having its own single and authoritative version. (The same may be said concerning the community that produced the Book of Jubilees.) Impartial historians cannot be sure of any text's being the original one. But the adherents of each text have no such doubts. They are convinced that theirs is the only true text, and hence the original. Within each group, deviation is discouraged if not condemned, and each group insists upon a single canonized text that suffers no serious changes.

If one traces the history of the biblical text across communities, one may arrive at no conclusion as to its original form. Too many communities compete for this title. If, however, one is tracing the history of the text within a particular group, one may reach a conclusion as to the emergence of that group's particular version, the history of that text's canonization, and, if the tradition endured for a long enough time, one may discern slight and inadvertent changes within the canonized text itself.[22]

Inconsistencies of Law

According to the narrative of Ezra and Nehemiah, the people of Israel no sooner heard the Law proclaimed than they went forth and began to observe its statutes. The narrator of Israel's religious rebirth in the book of Nehemiah seems eager to illustrate that the returned exiles translated their newly recovered Torah into practice. Here again, I shall quote the book of Nehemiah at length for its dramatic testimony, and for convenience, so that the reader may refer to this passage throughout the subsequent analysis.

On the second day, the heads of the ancestral houses of all the people, with the Priests and the Levites, came together to the scribe Ezra in order to study the words of the Law. And they found it written in the Law, which the Lord had commanded by Moses, that the people of Israel should live in booths during the festival of the seventh month, and that they should publish and proclaim in all their towns and in Jerusalem as follows: "Go out to the hills and bring branches of wild olive, myrtle, palm and other leafy trees to make booths, as it is written." So the people went out and brought them, and made booths for themselves, each on the roofs of their houses, and in the courts of the house of God, and in the square at the Water Gate and in the square at the Gate of Ephraim. And all the assembly of those who had returned from the captivity made booths and lived in them; for from the days of Joshua son of Nun to that day the people of Israel had not done so. And there was a very great rejoicing. And day by day, from the first day to the last day, he read from the book of the Law of God. They kept the festival seven days; and on the eighth day there was a solemn assembly, according to the ordinance. (Neh. 8:13–18)

In this account, the people appear to adjust their behavior to the Torah as soon as it is read aloud. The eagerness and zeal to observe God's commandments is evident in the words of the text. As soon as the people "found it written in the Law," they went forth to observe the festival. Scholars have debated the correlation between the materials listed in the passage above, for the building of the booths, and the species (fruit of goodly trees, branches of palm, and boughs of leafy trees), which in Leviticus 23:40 Israel was commanded to take in hand "and rejoice before the Lord." Are the accounts contradictory, as some critics believe, and thus indicative of separate sources? Or are we to understand, with the Samaritans and the Karaites, that Ezra and his congregation interpreted the commandment in Leviticus to mean that those materials were to be used, not for ritual waving, but for building the booths themselves? The latter position does not account for the discrepancies in number and species between the lists in Leviticus and Ezra. So we might turn to the rabbinic interpretation: that some of the species listed in the book of Ezra were gathered for a ritual taking-in-hand, and some for the building of booths. In any case, Ezra and his entourage evidently believed they were carrying out God's written will and proceeded to do so as swiftly as was feasible.

Yet the canonical Pentateuch, on its own, is not a book that lends itself to such easy and immediate application. Both modern and traditional scholarship have noted in their respective ways that the text of the Pentateuch contains apparent inconsistencies, gaps, and even contradictions, sometimes in the most essential matters of observance. In fact, the questions raised by the account of Ezra's Festival of Booths, cited above, serve to illustrate this point. The problem is not only that the laws of the festivals and Sabbaths are nowhere detailed enough that they might immediately be put into practice, as described in Nehemiah 8, without extensive guidance beyond the written word. Even more challenging than the frequent lack of detail is the fact that those details that are spelled out are not always congruous from one part of the Pentateuch to the other; moreover, those details are sometimes not at all consistent with the observances that are known to have been required in practice.

A short list of some representative inconsistencies will suffice to reveal the difficulties that must, inevitably, have presented themselves as the people of Israel encountered their Torah. According to Exodus 13:13, on the subject of unclean animals, only the firstlings of an ass must be redeemed with the offering of a lamb. However Numbers 18:15 dictates, "The firstlings of unclean animals shall you redeem," with no limitations. According to Exodus 21:7, "When a man sells his daughter as a slave, she shall not go out as the male slaves do." Deuteronomy 15:17, however, states that a female slave must be handled just as a male. Following Numbers 18:26, one would present the agricultural tithe to the Levites, but Leviticus 27:30 states that it must go to the priests alone. The Levitical law (Lev. 12:1–13) appears to assign the Passover rite to the home, whereas Deuteronomy 16:2 consigns it to the Temple grounds alone. Among more general inconsistencies, one may mention Exodus 20:24, which seems to permit sacrifice in any locale, though the entire Deuteronomic and postexilic corpus, as noted, inveighs against this practice.

These are but the most prominent of the apparent discrepancies, but even these are sufficient to demonstrate that coherent observance at the time of canonization cannot have been based on the scriptures alone. Some oral guidance must have accompanied the text as soon as observance was instituted, for even if we accept the rabbinic resolutions of these difficulties as expressive of the text's true meaning, these interpretations are often not sufficiently self-evident to be extrapolated without guidance. Rabbinic solutions to such problems are often too sophisticated to occur to the unschooled reader or listener. The Torah, however, unlike other law books, was intended to be read aloud before the people, and their cooperation would be solicited. As we have seen in the book of Nehemiah, public readings of the scriptures inspired a zeal for observance. The text must have been made accessible in more than just a general way, and the inevitable puzzlement of the listeners must have been addressed. The peasant who heard the text read aloud, or who was literate enough to read it—and who intended to prepare a Passover lamb, for example—would have been confounded by the contradictions if there had not been some additional information telling him how to behave and explaining why one verse was to take precedence over another. Explicit instructions alone cannot have been enough. As the text itself was read and heard, some explanation had to be made for the passages effectively displaced or altered by specifications found elsewhere in the canon. Such problems necessitate recourse to an authoritative oral tradition. Furthermore, it is not mere speculation to suggest that these discrepancies in the scriptures were, in fact, a pressing issue at the time of canonization. We have evidence within the Bible itself that suggests that these problems were perceived and addressed by the scribes and leaders of the postexilic age.

Evidence of Resolution in the Bible

It is well known that rabbinic interpretation reconciles apparent contradictions in the scriptures. Less well known is the fact that R. Ishmael acknowledged contradictions and—unlike the method sometimes attributed to his colleague, R. Akiba—did not reconcile them through mutual compromise but (as recited in the daily prayers) weighed *(machria)* two verses against each other with the help of a third, followed the two that he found to be in agreement, and consigned the remaining verse to a nonliteral interpretation. The last of R. Ishmael's thirteen tenets of exegesis states, "If two biblical passages contradict each other, they can be determined only by a third passage." Scarcely mentioned is the fact that this rabbinic principle appears to have its roots in biblical times.

The two books of Chronicles are late biblical texts, attributed by tradition to Ezra the Scribe and dated by critical scholarship to the early postexilic age. In describing the Passover sacrifice, the Chronicles (2 Chr. 35:13) employs an awkward Hebrew construction, declaring that the flesh was "cooked" (from the root *bshl*) in the fire. *Bshl* is elsewhere understood to denote boiling, and fire is associated with roasting. The phrase is unaccountably strange until we consider that Exodus 12:9 requires the paschal flesh to be roasted in fire, whereas Deuteronomy 16:7 employs the verb "*bshl*." Evidently the verse in Chronicles is an attempt to reconcile the two prescriptions, effectively subsuming one within the other.

A similar mediation between conflicting passages in the Pentateuch is indicated by 2 Chronicles 35:7–9. There, the dictum of Exodus 12:5, "You may take it [the Passover offering] from the sheep or from the goats," appears to have been reconciled with Deuteronomy 16:2, "You shall slaughter the Passover sacrifice for the Lord your God from the flock or from the herd." The resolution points toward the rabbinic conclusion that lambs and kids are to be employed for the Passover flesh itself, and animals from the herd are to be used for a supplementary *chagigah* contribution. In verse 7 of the passage in Chronicles, the author places the phrase "all of them for the Passover offerings" after the mention of Josiah's contribution of lambs and kids (from the flock) and before the mention of bullocks (from the herd), conveying the idea that the bullocks were not to be offered as the Passover offering itself, but as additional celebratory *(chagigah)* feasts. Also, the Masoretic text (verses 8 and 9) attaches the number of animals to the bullocks and only indirectly to the lambs and kids—another indication that the flock and the herd are to be employed in different functions, the former in paschal offerings and the latter in celebratory feasts. The *Mekhilta* employs the aforementioned method of R. Ishmael explicitly in handling the discrepancy:

> One scriptural verse says "And you should sacrifice the Passover offering . . . of the flock and the herd." And another scriptural verse says: "from the sheep or from the goats you shall take it." How can both these verses be maintained? There is a rule about the interpretation of the Torah: Two verses opposing one another . . . stand as they are until a third verse comes and decides between them. That verse is "Draw out and take your lambs according to your families and slaughter the Passover lamb."—From the flock only and not from the herd may the Passover offering come.[23]

The deciding factor in this scriptural quandary seems to have been Exodus 12:21, which states, "Pick out lambs for your families and slaughter the Passover offering." Here, no mention of "the herd" is made. The final decision is determined by the agreement of two verses, which, in turn, necessitates a nonliteral interpretation of a third. The contradiction is not clearly resolved, but a rule for observance is established. The fact that this rabbinic resolution is anticipated in the Chronicles demonstrates that such conflicts themselves were, in fact, an issue of concern at a time when the Bible itself was still unfolding. The corrective function of the passages in Chronicles raises two questions of central importance in understanding the period of canonization. First, we must ask how a decision was made between the prescriptions of Exodus and Leviticus. Second, given the prerogative of the Chronicler to record such a decision, we must ask why the text of the Pentateuch was not emended accordingly to bring it into consonance with actual practice.

The Existence of Oral Law

In answering the first question—how the decision between the conflicting prescriptions was made—two alternatives may be proposed. On the one hand, one might suggest that such decisions and details were a matter of personal choice, left to the individual adherent, who, having heard the scriptures read, was free to decide what they really meant. This suggestion would mean that the practical details of observance would not have been a matter of strict law but rather one of free-style interpretation. In this case, the resolutions indicated by the Chronicles would represent, not a priori decisions, but accounts, after the fact, of what the people had chosen to do. The other alternative is to posit that some authoritative determinant, beyond the written text, was responsible for consistent and coherent behavior.

Only the second alternative is plausible in context. The first suggestion is clearly incongruous with the spirit of the postexilic times as evidenced by the books of Ezra and Nehemiah. Given the recorded zeal of the people to hear authoritative guidance, repent their sins, and adhere to the God-given law, it is scarcely conceivable that contradictory pronouncements and open choices could have satisfied the nation at large, much less the religious leadership. The underlying motive in the compilation of the Law itself must have been the desire to create an enduring record of God's will. Contradictions and inconsistencies cannot have been appealing to the people. Nor can they have been untroubling to the stewards of the written law. To impute a tolerance of practical ambiguity in religion to the people of Ezra's day is to impose an altogether modern sensibility upon a time whose passion was for majestic and unchallenged law.

We must conclude that the leaders who presented the scriptural canon to Israel, in the manner described in Nehemiah 8, also gave explicit instructions as to how the text was to be employed. This function may well be documented by Nehemiah 8:7–8, in which Ezra's entourage aids the people in understanding the scriptural reading. The sacred text provides a powerful locus of divine authority, and the people rally around it; but the text itself requires adjunct explanation, and the religious leadership is able to provide the necessary instruction. In spite of textual maculations, coherent law is introduced.

An Analogy to the Mishnah

I have used evidence in the Bible itself to support the claim that despite the inconsistencies of the scriptures, the people received authoritative and unambiguous instruction. The scriptural discrepancies concerning the Passover offering had clearly been resolved by the time of the Chronicles' composition. The resolutions represented in the Chronicles point to the existence of instructions beyond the written word, instructions that allowed the people to overcome the apparent contradictions of the text. The indirect biblical evidence for such oral instruction is rather strong. The book of Nehemiah in particular contains many passages in which the religious leaders of the return from exile give instructions to the people, often paraphrasing the words of the scriptures. However, in the absence of more-explicit documentation of Ezra's means of providing oral instructions to the people, it is useful to employ analogy. We are faced with an inconsistent text and with evidence that the people knew what was required of them, despite scriptural maculation. This combination may seem less improbable in view of the problems of another age and another project of canonization.

A similar problem pertains to the rabbinic Mishnah, compiled by R. Judah Hanasi at the end of the second century. With regard to the Mishnah as well, scholars have disputed the significance of legal inconsistencies in the text. The Mishnah is a compendium of oral tradition on various subjects, transmitted through generations of rabbinic scholars whose rigorous attention to detail is famous and well documented. That the Mishnah records differences of opinion between the rabbis whose opinions it presents is in the nature of the work. Such inconsistencies of opinion are not flaws but are natural to the style and purpose of the Mishnah. However, the Mishnah served, not only as a record of opinions, but also as a code of law. The fact that it rarely states explicitly which of the statements in a series of conflicting opinions is to be taken as law does not mean that the Mishnah is nonfunctional as a law book. In fact, an elegant, unwritten system underlies the Mishnah's format and indicates the statements that were considered by the compiler as law. To understand this structural system completely, it is useful to review the contributions made to the Mishnah by its chief compiler, R. Judah Hanasi (also called Rabbi), who accomplished his work around the year 190. Rabbi's contribution to the Mishnah is twofold:

The Mishnah's Content.   Rabbi (and his court) decided the issues to be included in the Mishnah. That is not to say that Rabbi and his court assembled the Mishnah from scratch. It is very likely that the present Mishnah is simply the last in a line of pre- (or proto-) Mishnaic compilations, which probably resembled the Mishnah to a large extent in content and arrangement. Still, rabbinic dicta must have accumulated in the course of time, and that accumulation probably caused considerable changes in the content and layout of Rabbi's Mishnah from the *mishnaot* (or Mishnah-like compilations) that preceded his. The existence of proto-Mishnaic compilations is surmised, though there is no incontrovertible evidence for them. Indeed, except for a few quotations (like *"mishnah rishonah"* and *"ameru"*), we have little direct evidence of previous *mishnaot*. Indirect evidence, however, abounds. Many a statement in the Mishnah is cryptic, evidencing incomplete excerption. Such statements make sense only if we posit that an earlier proto-Mishnah contained a supplementary part or clause that would complete the excerpt found in Rabbi's Mishnah. That, however, remains in the realm of conjecture.

If, however, the preextant source of a *mishnah* is a *midrash halakha* (that is, an exegetical exposition of the law, based on scriptures) and if we discover the antecedent in one of those midrashic compilations that we do possess and are able thereby to complete a phrase in Rabbi's Mishnah, then the conjecture concerning previous *mishnaot* is strengthened. Let me cite two small examples. The Mishnah in Nazir 1:2 inquires, "How does a life-long Nazirite differ from a Nazirite like Samson?" and proceeds to explain the difference. The Babylonian Talmud (Nazir 4a) asks, "How does the life-long Nazirite come in here? (He was not mentioned yet)," and the Talmud explains, "There is a hiatus in the Mishnah and it should read as follows: 'If a man says, I intend to be a life-long Nazirite, he becomes a life-long Nazirite. What difference is there between a Nazirite like Samson and a life-long Nazirite?'" The compilation preceding the canonical Mishnah must have contained an extra phrase: "If a man says . . ." This sentence was omitted from our Mishnah, leaving the disjointed, incomplete discussion whose maculate nature is identified by the Babylonian Talmud.

The Mishnah Sukkah 4:8 reads: "The Hallel and the rejoicing eight days—what was the manner of this? This is to teach us *(melamed)* that a man is bound to recite the Hallel and observe the rejoicing . . . on the last festival day of the feast as on all other days of the feast." The sentence beginning "This is to teach us" does not answer the question, "What was the manner of this?" It seems to be an independent observation. Furthermore, the word *"melamed"* is a *terminus technicus,* found frequently in *midrashei halakha* and several times in the Mishnah, that is connected to a scriptural verse. It is clear, therefore, that the sentence beginning "This is to teach" comes from *midrash halakha,* with the scriptural proof text (answering the question, *"What* is to teach us?") omitted. The answer to the opening question, "What was the manner of this?" is also omitted and was probably found in an earlier Mishnah. Thus we have a lacuna in the text of the Mishnah consisting of an omission of a scriptural citation from a quoted *midrash halakha,* and of a question left hanging where once there must have been a recorded response. These examples demonstrate that the compilation of the present Mishnah was not a creation ex nihilo, but a work of anthology, drawing on previous compilations (and codifying several editorial errors).

One last example demonstrates rather elegantly that Rabbi's Mishnah followed previous compilations in content and in order. Our Mishnah's tractate Kelim ends with the saying of R. Yose: "Blessed are you O *Kelim,* for you begin in impurity and have concluded in purity." That is a reference to the first and the last segments of the tractate; the first begins, "These are the first sources of impurity," and the last ends with the word "pure." R. Yose lived and worked before Rabbi, and his statement was obviously composed before Rabbi's Mishnah itself. Therefore it is evident that the order of tractate Kelim was already established before Rabbi. It may be that Rabbi and his court added or rearranged some content; but if they did, they did so in a way that preserved R. Yose's statement and its validity. Rabbi's Mishnah is based on previous compilations; and yet Rabbi's work is definitive inasmuch as it canonized his particular version of the Mishnah with its own distinct features. Moreover, these distinct features are represented, not by content alone, but also by editorial choices in the arrangement of this content in the schematic structure of the Mishnah—Rabbi's second contribution.

The Mishnah's Form.   Rabbi also contributed an editorial scheme for the presentation of disputed issues. Again, this scheme probably followed the layout of previous Mishnah-like compilations, though no such corpora are extant for comparison. The schematic structure of the Mishnah may be described in brief as follows: Some rabbinic positions are recorded in anonymous opinions, which enjoy the highest authority. Others consist of anonymous opinions with an attributed dissenting view attached. The anonymous position still prevails, but its authority is somewhat compromised by the lack of unanimity. It is easier to overturn an anonymous position when dissenting views are in evidence in the Mishnah itself. Still other passages in the Mishnah contain series of dicta attributed to various Tannaitic rabbis. Positions recorded without attribution or attributed to "the Sages" are ones that were adopted by Rabbi's court as law, as a passage in the Babylonian Talmud (Chulin 85a) explains: "R. Hiyya bar Abba said in the name of R. Yochanan: Rabbi approved of R. Meir's view in connection with the law of 'it and its young' [a biblical prohibition against the sacrifice of an animal and its offspring on the same day] and codified it in the Mishnah as the view of 'the Sages'; and he approved of R. Simeon's view in connection with the covering of the blood and codified it in the Mishnah as the view of 'the Sages.'" With respect to anonymous views followed by attributed ones, the Mishnah itself, in Eduyot 1:4 explains: "Why do they record the opinion of the individual against that of the majority, whereas the *halakha* may be only according to the majority? That if a court [later] approves the opinion of the individual, it may rely upon him [i.e., it may know that there is a precedent and cite it]."

In connection with a series of attributed opinions, both Talmudim (Palestinian and Babylonian) also record general principles as to which rabbis' views are to be followed. It should be mentioned that none of these general principles is universally borne out in practice. Exceptions may be found to each of these rules—instances in which the halakha is not as we might expect—yet the exceptions are uncommon, and, in general, it may be concluded that the Mishnah's scheme was intended to convey a hierarchy of authority.

I must also mention that there are instances in which two dicta in the Mishnah's own anonymous voice (traditionally called *stam mishnah*) contradict each other explicitly. The most confirmed of these is a contradiction in the Mishnah's tractate Sukkah in the fourth and fifth *mishnaot* of the fifth chapter. The fourth *mishnah* says, "When they reached the tenth step (in the courtyard of the Temple) they (the two priests with trumpets in their hands) blew a sustained, a quavering, and another sustained blast." Mishnah five, however, states, "[They blew] three at the altar." We know from the Tosefta (Sukkah 4:10, quoted also in the Babylonian Talmud, Sukkah 54a, and in the Palestinian Talmud, Sukkah 55b) that "he who holds that the priests blew at the altar does not hold that they blew on the tenth step; and he who holds that they blew on the tenth step does not hold that they blew at the altar." The two positions are incompatible, and yet they are both expressed in the same voice, the anonymous persona of the Mishnah. We should note that some scholars still refuse to acknowledge even this passage in Sukkah as an outright contradiction in the Mishnah (despite the words of the Tosefta). Other instances of contradiction are so exceedingly rare that it is difficult to disabuse such scholars of the notion that the Mishnah is entirely perfect. In general, then, the schematic layout of the Mishnah is intended to convey law.

Nevertheless, the intention of the Mishnah to communicate the relative authority of its dicta is not documented explicitly in the Mishnah itself or in any preceding rabbinic document. Rather, this scheme and the other rules concerning the dicta to be followed are matters of oral law. As in the case of the Pentateuch and the entourage of Ezra, we must assume that R. Judah Hanasi and his circle were aware of the differences in dicta. With respect to the Mishnah, the compendium was meant to contain these differences. Moreover, it is also inconceivable that the more rare idiosyncratic inconsistencies (such as the passage in Sukkah, cited above) were overlooked by the scholars and students who codified and memorized the corpus entire.

Some modern scholars have claimed that these internal inconsistencies prove that the Mishnah was not intended to be used as a definitive code of law. This suggestion, however, is out of keeping with the explicit concerns of the Mishnah itself and with the rabbinic project in general. The determination and enforcement of definitive halakha is the fundamental goal of the Mishnah's jurisprudence, and the authority to pronounce authoritative law is the basis on which subsequent rabbinic dialectics are grounded. Consequently, we must conclude that there were ways and means in rabbinic circles to overcome the Mishnah's discrepancies. Rules or traditions must have accompanied rabbinic differences of opinion; if not, Talmudic lore would be improbably perched upon dubious foundations. Indeed, R. Yochanan, who was a disciple of R. Judah Hanasi, cited many rules for adducing practical law from the Mishnah; and it is unlikely that these rules were his own innovation. In fact, some such rules are of Tannaitic origin. The law always follows the Hillelites (over the Shamaites); does not follow R. Eliezer ben Hurkanos ("R. Eliezer Shemutihu"); always follows R.

Eliezer ben Yaakov (*kav venaki*, "few but clean"). According to Issi ben Judah, a late Tanna, R. Yose's views are always accepted *(nimukei imo)*. It is quite plausible that rules existed for deciding all such disputes, not only for a few.

The rabbis at the time of the Mishnah's codification were concerned with proper observance and with the accurate transmission of legal opinions. We know this from the codificatory system of the Mishnah, which quotes some opinions as majority views and some as minority positions. That distinction would be of little value if the intent were not to communicate practical law. In fact, the Mishnah itself (in Eduyot 1:5–6) explains why the rejected minority views were recorded: in order that future judges might reverse the rulings, which, apparently, they would be unable to do if no dissent were recorded. Despite several instances of textual incongruity in the Mishnah, which run against the spirit of its times, the people knew how to behave. These inconsistencies did not undermine the overall structure of the Mishnah or belie the rabbinic concern for accuracy and authoritative rulings. Instead, these maculations indicate that the rabbis knew how to deal with anomalous problems that had somehow entered the text. The rabbis did not allow these problems to cause uncertainty in the realm of actual practice.[24] Likewise, in the case of Ezra and his entourage at the time of the return from exile, the religious leadership was able to overcome the conflicting passages of its Holy Scriptures. The text of the canonical Pentateuch contains apparent inconsistencies; but the people of Israel knew how to behave nonetheless.

The Source of Oral Instruction

We have yet to explain how Ezra and his entourage, the religious leadership, were able to resolve the problems of the written text. On what basis did they dictate their authoritative oral guidelines when the scriptures were ambiguous or inconsistent? One might suggest that in cases of conflicting scriptures, the leadership made a choice based on some form of logic, reason, or even taste, giving precedence to one law over another according to the leaders' own sense of what was right. Possibly this suggestion could account for the overcoming of outright contradictions in the written law. We can imagine that even arbitrary decisions between conflicting passages might have been effective in eliminating ambiguity. But outright contradictions are by far not the only difficulties encountered by the compilers and promoters of the canonical Pentateuch. Rational, or even arbitrary, decisions between conflicting laws might explain coherent behavior in the face of outright contradictions in the written word. Yet we must still account for instances in which the written word was displaced without the aid of conflicting passages elsewhere in the text.

The interpretation of scriptural verses against their plain meaning *(lo kiphshutam)* is a well-known phenomenon in rabbinic exegesis. Although the present sources are exclusively rabbinic, it should not be assumed that all such interpretations are of rabbinic provenance originally. It seems inconceivable that the Tannaim, who considered the scriptures divine writ, demanding absolute devotion, suffering no deviation, could have displaced the plain meaning of a verse entirely; and yet some interpretations exclude the literal meaning of the verses they exposit. The only possible explanation is that in instances in which the apparent contextual meaning and legal import of a verse is flatly contravened by the verse's traditional exposition, the originators of the interpretation must have had certain knowledge that the text at that locus was unreliable. Otherwise, the plain meaning of scriptural words reigned supreme, embellished by, but never entirely displaced by, oral law. Only when the text itself was not secure, when its wording was regarded as suspect, could interpretations displace plain meaning entirely. Wanton and gratuitous displacements of plain scriptural meaning would have been branded as heresy.

By the time of the Tannaim, the several instances in which plain meaning, or *peshat,* is displaced by oral law were well established. Tannaitic arguments over these passages concern only the details of their implementation. The effective changes themselves are taken for granted. Aside from these accepted instances of displaced *peshat,* the text of the Pentateuch was no longer subject to the displacement of plain meaning. We may assume, then, that such displacements took place long before the period of the Tannaim, at a time when elements of the text itself were still in flux—that is to say, not much after the time of Ezra and his scribes. We need not look to the rabbinic age to find the earliest evidence that some words in the canon were considered less secure than others. The phenomenon of the *puncta extraordinaria,* mentioned at the beginning of this chapter, demonstrates that even the scribes of canonization themselves were aware of instances in which the wording of the text was probably unsound.

The ten *puncta extraordinaria* (in Hebrew, *eser nekudot*), as explained above, according to tradition, identify words and phrases whose rightful place in the text of the Pentateuch was questioned by the canonizers themselves. I have already made reference to the imagined dialogue between Ezra the Scribe and Elijah the Prophet (or Moses) (found in Bamidbar Rabbah and parallels) in which Ezra defends his decision to include suspect verses in the Pentateuch by noting that he has marked them accordingly. The phenomenon of the *eser nekudot* indicates an opposition of editorial inclinations. On the one hand, the passages marked by *nekudot* indicate an unwillingness on the part of the scribes to discard any part of their textual legacy, even when they were well aware of textual problems. On the other hand, the *nekudot* are audacious testimony, from the scribes themselves, that words and phrases have gone awry in the text.

It is very doubtful that any generation subsequent to that of Ezra himself might be responsible for the introduction of the *eser nekudot*. It is difficult to imagine that anyone subsequent to Ezra could have taken such liberties with the text. Moreover, we have the evidence of rabbinic tradition that ascribes these markings to Ezra, as noted in the passage from Bamidbar Rabbah. The introduction of visible markers of doubt within the written text was an audacious undertaking. It is unlikely that this innovation was the work of anyone with less power over the text than the canonizers themselves. As we shall see, the written Torah so swiftly assumed the ultimate religious sanctity that it is hard to imagine any subsequent generation presuming to impose upon it these extraordinary markings of suspicion. It is clear then that the very same leaders who were responsible for the promotion of the written text were also the stewards of an oral tradition that governed both their treatment of this text and the instructions that they gave the people.

What is true of the *puncta extraordinaria* is also true of the contradictions in the written law and of those instances in which the plain meaning of scriptures is superseded by rabbinic law. We are dealing here with instances in which the plain meaning of a verse is displaced entirely by the behavior required in practice. In some cases, the apparent meaning of a passage was annulled through the decision to follow a contradictory scripture. In other cases, the plain meaning was displaced without such a motivating factor within the Pentateuch itself. Instances of the latter kind are exemplified by the *eser nekudot*.

As to the few instances in the literature of the Mishnaic rabbis, the Tannaim, in which the plain meaning of a verse is displaced entirely, it is most likely that these departures from *peshat* date back to the time of Ezra, for only then would anybody have dared to abandon the plain meaning of the text. The scriptures explicitly demand "an eye for an eye," and yet the earliest rabbis take for granted that pecuniary compensation is required. Regarding levirate marriage, the scriptures state clearly, "And the first son whom she bears shall succeed in the name of his brother who is dead" (Deut. 25:6). According to the plain meaning of the verse, the first son of the widowed woman, by her new husband, succeeds in the name of the deceased former husband (the brother of the new spouse). The early rabbis, however, interpreted the verse as though it read, "the eldest son *who was born* shall inherit in the name of his brother," requiring that the eldest brother of the deceased man enter the levirate marriage. Leviticus 7:18 states unambiguously, "And if any of the flesh of [a man's] peace-offerings be eaten on the third day [instead of on the required first two days], it shall not be accepted, neither shall it be imputed unto him that offereth it; it shall be an abhorred thing and the soul that eats thereof shall bear his iniquity." The early rabbis, however, insist that the text is referring to a priest who, while performing the ritual slaughter, intends to eat the flesh on the third day. If the priest had no such intentions at the time of the slaughter itself, the rabbis contend, then even if he partakes of the flesh on the third day, the sacrifice is not invalidated. These examples do not represent gratuitous departures from *peshat* on the part of the rabbis. Rather, the anomalies are a sign of rabbinic fealty to instructions handed down with the written text from the very time of its compilation.

The argument above should not be construed as implying that after canonization, the Pentateuch became entirely monolithic, with no changes at all occurring over time. In fact, textual variants within any one segment of early Judaism, not to mention textual differences among sects, are too numerous and too well known to warrant listing. It is clear that human transmission through the ages, even after canonization, gave rise to scribal errors and other inconsistencies, even within the Masoretic tradition. At the end of this chapter, instances in which even rabbinic quotations of scriptures departed from the canonical written word will be discussed. Nevertheless, none of these inconsistencies, however introduced, involved divergences between the written word and the meaning attributed to it. The meaning remained faithful to the text. No incongruity arose between the two.

Most likely, the changes that arose after Ezra's canonization were introduced unwittingly, unperceived by scribe or reader. When a text is altered inadvertently, the meaning changes along with the text (otherwise, the tension between text and intended meaning would result in the error's being noticed). Such unperceived changes certainly occurred even after canonization. Changes are in the nature of things, and despite public readings and other precautionary measures, the text did not escape inadvertent alterations. Such deviations could happen at any time (especially before printing and the wide circulation of text).

My concern here, however, is with acknowledged discrepancies between literal and imputed meaning, between what the text apparently says, and the way we are asked to understand it. Such incompatibilities could not have arisen spontaneously after a protracted period of agreement between text and meaning. The open flouting of apparent meaning, and flaunting of nonliteral interpretations that displace this meaning entirely, can occur only when the written word itself is insecure and does not command the same adherence as text that is regarded without suspicion. Let me present an example from the case of levirate marriage, mentioned above. It is quite conceivable that somebody could unwittingly have exchanged the words "who was borne" *(asher nolad)* with "whom she shall bear" *(asher teled)*. In Hebrew the orthographic difference is not great. Such a change is conceivable in any period, early or late. In this case, however, in which the law, as actually observed, does not follow the written word *(asher teled)* but ignores the literal meaning entirely and points to a previous version *(asher nolad),* I contend that the scriptural alteration took place prior to Ezra's time. As shall be explained below, the maculated text *(asher teled)* was preserved in canonization, even as the original meaning of the lost scripture *(asher nolad)* was taught in practice, following an oral tradition.

At this point we must return to the *eser nekudot* and stress that these markings are strong evidence for the existence of a comprehensive oral tradition beyond the written word, passed down from a time before the canonization of Ezra's day. The *nekudot* indicate that Ezra and his entourage did not resort to oral instruction only when the scriptures were contradictory. Rather, the entire Pentateuch seems to have been compared to some standard of accuracy beyond the scriptures themselves. As has been noted, the resolution of contradictions might be accounted for by the prerogatives of leadership alone. The *nekudot,* however, indicate that these prerogatives were coupled with an oral tradition of the highest authority that Ezra and his entourage inherited from their forebears. Thus, with respect to the compilation undertaken by Ezra, one must conclude that above and beyond the scriptures themselves, an extratextual tradition served as a standard by which maculations in the text were identified and overcome. Since this oral, or extratextual, tradition evidently was able to displace the very text that was revered as the legacy of Sinai, it is possible, and perhaps necessary, to conclude that Ezra and his entourage saw their oral standard as the true content of the revelation to Moses in the desert, passed down to them through the judges and the prophets.

The Inviolability of Text

I have said that Ezra and his entourage of scribes and priests pronounced unambiguous laws, marked suspect passages, and resolved textual contradictions. They were able to do so on the basis of their own heritage of authoritative oral tradition. The period of return from exile was indeed characterized by the zeal for detailed law described in the books of Ezra and Nehemiah. Moreover, evidence has been shown that the religious leadership of the return from exile was able to provide the people with authoritative guidance. The narratives in Ezra and Nehemiah and in the Chronicles, describing the observance of the festivals, indicate that there was uniform, organized behavior, not just chaotic enthusiasm. The people were told what to do, and the instructions were unambiguous.

Following biblical and rabbinic evidence, I also have concurred that this period saw the compilation of the scriptural law in its present canon. Yet this canon preserves textual inconsistencies that are a challenge to coherent observance. These inconsistencies, however, do not require that we modify our appreciation of the postexilic spirit. In fact, there is sufficient evidence to understand just why a maculated Pentateuch was canonized even as authoritative oral law emerged in practice.

If the purveyors of the canonical Torah were also in possession of knowledge and tradition that allowed them to displace or suspect the written word, why did they not employ their editorial prerogative to correct the written word? The only possible answer is that they had no such prerogative. For the scribes of canonization themselves, the written word was sacred and inviolable.

Thus, remarkably, the persisting maculations of the Holy Scriptures are themselves the strongest evidence that the canonical Pentateuch was assembled from textual traditions that were regarded by their stewards as holy and beyond correction. The uneven text of the Pentateuch, the *eser nekudot,* and the displacement of the written word in actual practice all indicate that Ezra and his scribes were aware of problems in the text. Nevertheless, the fact that these maculations were allowed to remain in place indicates that the scribes themselves had reverence for the scriptures they had inherited. The entourage of Ezra was aware that centuries of imperiled textual transmission, through dangerous and hostile times, had made them heirs to a troubled scriptural inheritance. Yet we can be sure that these canonizers were also convinced that their scriptures were the legacy of Sinai, that their Torah was beyond reproach.

An Analogy to Jeremiah: Kilkul Cheshbonot

For Ezra and his entourage, the written Book of the Law seems to have functioned as a symbolic banner under which the people of Israel were united in religion. For the scribes of canonization, the scriptures were the best available remnants of the events at Sinai, and Ezra and his scribes arranged them in the best possible order, marking the text itself in extreme cases of doubt. For the people themselves, the book that Ezra opened before the assembly was the Torah of Moses, the actual content of revelation. According to the account in Nehemiah, the Torah's appearance was so powerful that the people stood as one and united their hearts in repentance and resolve. To have asserted a prerogative to impose changes upon the written text would have undermined the majesty and power of the scriptures, even if they might thereby have been rendered more coherent and complete. In principle, the tangible sign of revelation, the Torah, had to be perfect. In practice, therefore, its imperfections were circumvented and allowed to remain in place.

An analogue to this situation may be found in the account of Jerusalem's fall, as told by Jeremiah, and in the rabbinic laws that prescribe commemorations of the event. To this day, a fast is observed on the seventeenth day of Tammuz, marking the date on which the walls of Jerusalem were breached. When we turn to Jeremiah (52:6), however, we find that the date given for this event by this purportedly first-hand source is the ninth of the month, not the seventeenth. The earliest rabbis were not oblivious of the contradictory scripture, and yet the nonscriptural tradition remained in place in practice. Both Talmudim take up the problem, and each resolves it differently. According to the Babylonian Talmud (Taanit 28b), the date of the seventeenth of Tammuz commemorates the breach of the walls of the Second Temple, and the ninth day commemorates the breach of the First Temple walls, as recorded in Jeremiah. The fast, then, is observed in connection with the Second Temple. This solution, however, leaves unanswered the question of why a nonscriptural date, pertaining ostensibly to the Second Temple, is observed, whereas a written date, connected to the First Temple, is neglected entirely.

The Palestinian Talmud (Taanit 68c, in the name of R. Tanchum bar Chanilai, a third-century Palestinian scholar) presents a solution that, although far more radical, is more plausible historically. R. Tanchum insisted that the fast be observed on the seventeenth day, according to the oral tradition. Turning to the written record, R. Tanchum declared that the anomalous date in Jeremiah was the result of *kilkul cheshbonot,* "an error in calculation." The Judeans of Jeremiah's time, according to R. Tanchum, had more pressing matters at hand than the painful reconstruction of the calendar of Jerusalem's fall. Thus an actual error, R. Tanchum maintained, was encoded in the biblical record. It goes without saying that no change was imposed upon the wording of the book of Jeremiah. In spite of the imputed error, alteration of the text would be utter sacrilege. One does not tamper with the canonical record of a prophet. Jeremiah or his scribe may have been in error, as far as the actual date of the commemoration is concerned; but Jeremiah's prophetic stature and the canonical inviolability of his book stand above correction.

The Rabbinic Scriptures and the Masoretic Text

Further discrepancies between rabbinic tradition and the canonical scriptures are found in the many conflicting readings between the Masoretic text of the Pentateuch (the version of the Torah read aloud in the synagogue) and the citations of the Torah in rabbinic literature. Despite some modern demurral, the evidence is overwhelming that such conflicts are not infrequent and that many Rishonim (medieval Talmudic commentators) alluded to this problem specifically or were at least aware of its presence without seeing cause for theological alarm.

A short example of such a discrepancy will suffice. The Babylonian Talmud (Kiddushin 66b) quotes R. Judah in the name of Shemuel as saying that the scriptural source for the law that states that a service performed by a blemished priest is invalid is the passage, "Behold, I give him my covenant in perfection *[shalem]*"—that is, when the priest is perfect, but not when he is blemished. The scriptural verse, however, reads "in peace" *(shalom),* and not "in perfection" *(shalem).* In the ensuing Talmudic discussion, R. Nachman explains that the *vav* of *"shalom"* is broken off in the middle, so that it might be read as *(shalem).* However, in the canonical text, the *vav* is *not* broken off, so that the law concerning a blemished priest appears to have no scriptural basis.

Indeed, some commentators took note of such discrepancies between rabbinic quotations and scriptural texts without even seeing fit to explain why no theological problem arises from following both rabbinic and Masoretic readings in practice. Those commentators posited mutuality and were confident that future generations would not see in these conflicts irreconcilable antagonisms, even though the discrepancies affect not only narrative passages, without legal consequences, but also legal passages with direct implications for actual behavior, and even though, to put it most bluntly, if we were to write out a scroll of the Torah, following the scriptural citations of the rabbinic texts, this scroll would be ritually invalid for use in the synagogue. Such a scroll would depart in word and phrase from the canonical Masoretic text. Even so, it is the rabbinic citations, not the canonical scriptures, that are followed in matters of practice. Just as the rabbinic version of the Torah would be sacrilegious in a ritual reading, many specifications of the Masoretic text would be considered sacrilege if employed in practice. No lesser an authority than the Rashba (1235–1310) attempted to overcome the discrepancies, suggesting that the Masoretic readings be corrected according to the rabbinic laws. However, the Rashba did not succeed in displacing the divergent scriptural passages. The laws of the Talmud are followed, of course, but the scribes, to this day, follow the Masoretic text. The inviolability of text prevailed.

Another indication of the inviolability of text may be extracted from the rabbinic statement found in the *Sifra Achrei,* 6:2 (p. 82b, Weiss edition), P.T. Yoma 44a, B.T. Yoma 32a (and parallels). I am quoting the Babylonian Talmud:

> Our rabbis taught [a Tannaitic source]: "And Aaron shall come into the tent of meeting and put off his linen vestments . . . and bathe his body in water" (Lev. 16:23)—for what purpose does he enter? For no other purpose than that of taking out the censer and the coal pan (left there when he entered the holy of holies), the whole sequence being reported in the correct order with the exception of this passage. For what reason? R. Hisda said: There is a tradition that the high priest underwent five immersions and ten sanctifications. If he had performed them in the order listed in the scriptures, there could have been no more than three immersions and six sanctifications.

Without going into the details of why, had we followed the order of scriptures, the immersions would have to be reduced from five to three and the sanctifications from ten to six; it suffices in this book to point out that because of a *tradition*, the rabbis declared a scriptural verse to be out of sequence. (By this interpretation, the verse should occur where verse 28 is, rather than 23.) And, of course, despite its being in the wrong place, the verse was not moved to its proper place. Inviolability of the text precludes such corrections. One may, of course, question whether an explanation given by a third-century Babylonian Amora for a Tannaitic statement about the misplacement of a verse is necessarily accurate. Indeed, some commentators claim that the verse in its present location would be untenable even if it were not contradicted by an oral tradition. It is extremely unlikely that the high priest would have disrobed and bathed *in* the tent of meeting. Something needs to be added to the substance of the present text that might itself shed light upon the proper order of the verses. Most likely, there were also other reasons, besides the tradition of five immersions and ten sanctifications, that contributed to this verse's being declared out of place.

Whatever the reason, the text must have been lacunal from a very early stage, during which time nobody dared to correct it and restore the verse to its proper place. The inviolability of the text was honored even while the illogicality of its present place was being acknowledged. The rabbis found no theological offense in this dichotomy. True, some scholars, from R. Yose (the Amora, in P.T. Yoma 44a) to the Gaon of Vilna (1720–1797), apparently felt theologically uncomfortable with this declaration and attempted, without success, to show that the verse *is* in the proper order. Nonetheless, the overwhelming majority of rabbinic scholars throughout the ages, including Rashi in his commentary on the Pentateuch, accepted the idea that the verse was out of place and were not troubled by that or by the question of why its lacuna was not corrected. These rabbis must have respected a concept of textual inviolability, an awareness that lacunae must remain unchanged in order not to disturb the sanctity of the written word.

In connection with verses or phrases not being in the right order, let me mention the hermeneutical principle of *"im eino inyan legufo, teneino inyan l'"*—"if it has no bearing on its own subject, apply it elsewhere." In certain instances, the application to another matter is *complete*—the verse retains no meaning in its written place, and the law in that place is interpreted accordingly. The question then arises—in contrast with instances in which the application to another matter is not complete and the verse retains meaning in *both* connections—why are verses that retain no meaning in their present context not physically transposed to their proper matter? I shall cite briefly the oldest example (with roots already in the book of Nehemiah) from the *Mekhilta*[25] and from the *Sifrei* on Numbers: Numbers

18:15 says in part, "And the firstlings of unclean beasts you shall redeem," whereas, according to Exodus 13:13, only the firstlings of an ass must be redeemed. The Midrash resolves the contradiction by applying the principle of "im eino inyan legufo, teneino l'" to the phrase in Numbers, saying, "If it has no bearing on the subject of redeeming the firstlings of unclean animals, consider it as bearing upon the consecration of unclean beasts for the temple repairs—that one should redeem them if they have been so consecrated." The Midrash transfers the phrase in Numbers 18:15, "And the firstlings of unclean beasts you shall redeem," to another subject—one whose place is Leviticus 27:27. We must then ask why, if the phrase was deemed to have no bearing where it is, it was not physically transposed into its proper place. The answer must be the inviolability of the text. The maculate text was too entrenched to have been altered.

A similar phenomenon seems to be presented by both Talmudim (B.T. Baba Kama 107a and P.T. Baba Kama 36b), in connection with Exodus 22:8. According to these sources, there is here an "interweaving of sections" *(eiruv parshiot),* as the words "this is it" (in Exodus 22:8) are said with reference to loans (and thus pertain to Exodus 22:24). Why then were these words not transferred to their proper context?[26] Again the answer is the inviolability of text. Because of neglect (and the phenomenon of *Chate'u Yisrael,* Israel's indulgence in idolatry), by the time of Ezra and his school the text of the Pentateuch had been maculate for quite some time. Textual inviolability precluded physical correction; instead of textual emendation, corrective oral traditions arose concerning scriptural maculations. The Talmudic sources cited above claim to be just such traditions.

In a few places in the Talmud[27] the rabbis employ the principle of *"sirus,"* transposing the order of the words in a passage. Let me cite first one example from the *Mekhilta,* tractate Vayisa 4 (p. 116 in Lauterbach's edition): "'And it bred worms and rotted' (Ex. 16:20). The order in this passage is to be transposed, for does a thing first breed worms and then rot? It is but after it rots that it breeds worms." Here the transposition may be intended more as an accompanying commentary than as a statement that something is wrong with the written text. Let me also cite another example, from B.T. Sotah 38a: "'In every place where I cause my name to be remembered, I will come to you and bless you' (Ex. 20:24). Can it enter your mind that 'every place' is intended? Rather, the text must be transposed: 'In every place where I will come to you and bless you, I will cause my name to be remembered.'" But if the order of the passage is wrong[28] and requires transposition, why was the text not corrected? Again, textual inviolability precludes that. Even if it is a mistake, once it entered the canon, it became impossible to dislodge.

The Talmud also says, in the name of some Amoraim, that "one may subtract [a letter from one word], add [it to another] and interpret" *(Gorin umosifin vedorshin).*[29] However, that may not indicate that the letters are in the wrong place to begin with; only that an additional *derash,* an extra exposition, can be gained by manipulating the letters thus.[30]

Mention should also be made of *tikkun soferim,* an emendation of the *soferim* (the scribes).[31] R. Simon (a third-century Palestinian scholar), who is quoted in *Midrash Rabbah,* Genesis 49:7 (ed. Theodor Albeck, p. 505), as saying: "'but Abraham stood before the Lord' (Gen. 8:22)—this is an emendation of the *soferim,* for the Shekhinah was actually waiting for Abraham," apparently did not see religious incongruity in the notion that the *soferim,* the people of the High Synod, of which traditionally Ezra was a member, emended the Pentateuchal text.[32] However, this idea did bother the Rashba, as he is quoted by R. E. Mizrahi (d. ca. 1525) on Genesis 18:22; and it bothered a host of others up to our own day (among them also the Maharal in his *Gur Arryeh,* ad. loc.). "God forbid," says the Rashba, "that the *soferim* would add or change what is written in the Torah." To him, and to the others, that was a theological impossibility.

We have again observed a phenomenon that at first appears improbable, but then proves a commonplace in the history of Jewish tradition. In spite of what the sensibilities of twentieth-century literacy and criticism may tell us, it is possible for a people to venerate scriptures that speak in one way while, in practice, behaving in another way and even intimating that the scriptural text is maculate. This dichotomy is manifest in the rabbinic citations of the scriptural text and in the rabbinic treatment of Jeremiah's ninth of Tammuz, as well as in the other examples cited above. This argument suggests that such a dichotomy was possible, and even necessary, *at the time of canonization itself.* That accounts for the inclusion in the scriptures of the rejected dicta, which inevitably remain when contradictory passages are followed. This phenomenon also accounts for the persistence of the spurious letters or words marked by the *eser nekudot.* We are also now in a position to account for the unusual instances in which rabbinic literature displaces entirely the plain meaning of a text, mandating a practice that is incompatible with the literal meaning of the scriptural words. In all of those cases, the maculated text retains its sanctity despite its practical inapplicability.

Keri *and* Ketiv

Mention should also be made of the frequent differences between *keri* and *ketiv,* between the way a word appears in the text and the way it is read aloud in a public ritual reading. These discrepancies sometimes have practical, halakhic implications. The number of walls required in the building of a sukkah, for example, depends, in the Talmudic dispute (B.T. Sukkah 6a; Sanhedrin 4a), upon whether one regards the *keri* or the *ketiv* as determinative. According to Rabbi Shimon, one follows the *keri (yesh em lamikra),* and consequently three; according to the Sages, one follows the *ketiv (yesh em lamasorah),* and therefore two. The origin of these differences between orthography and reading is not clear. Although I cannot find sufficient evidence to take a firm stand on the dating of these discrepancies, they may be used to illustrate some of the points made above. On the one hand, the problem of *keri* and *ketiv* demonstrates the principle of the inviolability of text. Even as altered readings *(keri)* effectively superseded the scriptural orthography, these readings did not displace the written words themselves. The scriptures maintained their form, and the divergent readings were transmitted as an oral tradition, adjunct to the preserved holy text.

R. David Kimchi (the Radak, 1160–1235), in the introduction to his commentary on the book of Joshua, presented an opinion endorsed by some of the great halakhic scholars of the late Middle Ages. Kimchi stated that the differences arose in the confusion of exile and that Ezra and his entourage, when they returned, were so much in doubt about the correct orthography that they instituted the system of *keri* and *ketiv.* This, of course, implies a degree of ambiguity between the read and the written forms. Nevertheless, even when a written word is not read as it is written, the holy status of the word in the scriptural text is not diminished. The scriptures maintain, uniformly, the status of divine writ. Even if the *keri* is the version followed in practice, displacing the *ketiv* by writing the *keri* instead would render a scroll of the Torah ritually invalid.

The Radak's opinion places the ambiguity between *keri* and *ketiv* in the period of exile and attributes the transmission of both forms to Ezra himself. Some, however, may also say that instances of *keri* and *ketiv* arose through the gradual and accidental accumulation of errata in the text, following canonization. If a word was recorded in error, following a scribal error or an error of mistaken hearing, the altered text might have been circulated and accepted as holy writ before the error became apparent. Someone with a knowledge of the previous, unaltered text might then have noticed the discrepancy. Even so, the altered text could not be replaced, since conscious tampering with the written word would not have been acceptable. Therefore the previous, unaltered text would have been reintroduced, at a later date, as an adjunct oral tradition, to be pronounced aloud as a *keri*, but not to displace the written word, the *ketiv.* Alternatively, it may have happened that a small group within the chain of textual transmission somehow unwittingly introduced alterations in its text. Over time, this divergence from the textual mainstream may have resulted in two or more subtly different versions of the canon, circulating at the same time. The variant readings of either group may then have been added marginally to the text of the other, as *keri*, leaving the text in place as *ketiv.*

Obviously, there are many possible permutations in such accidents of history. Moreover, as a result of such mishaps, there may well have been times in which uncertainty arose regarding the correct orthography. For this reason, and because we lack detailed evidence, we cannot conclude that either the *keri* or the *ketiv* consistently represents the "correct" text, whereas the other preserves errata. The same problem, evidently, was faced by the early rabbis, who argued over the respective authority of the *keri* and *ketiv,* as already shown, with some rabbis upholding the *keri,* and some the *ketiv.*

Ezra's Project in Review

Let us review our argument thus far. Modern critical methodologies have identified multiple strands and strata within the scriptural Torah. Whatever one makes of these academic findings—whatever chronology one imputes to the text—the literal surface of the Pentateuch, as it was canonized, provides challenging instances of inconsistency and other apparent maculation. We have even seen that the rabbis of the Talmud recognize certain maculations in the Pentateuch and indeed acknowledge, with systematic corrective devices, the following types of problem: (1) that there are words or phrases requiring erasure (marked by the points or *nekudot*), (2) that there are words that must not be read according to their orthography (*keri* and *ketiv*), and (3) that there are passages and phrases that are in the wrong place (*eiruv parshiot* and *im eino inyan legufo* . . .). Moreover, the rabbis cite the phenomenon of *kilkul cheshbonot* (an error in calculation) to explain the deviation of scripture and practice, and they occasionally quote verses in versions that depart from the written word.

All of these rabbinic tactics acknowledge, to varying degrees, maculation in the text. It seems that this acknowledgment did not generate theological difficulties—at least we have no record of such difficulties. The earliest interpreters probably were more inclined than we might suppose to admit that centuries of transmission and crisis had allowed flaws to enter into the text. In fact, there is evidence that suggests that such flaws may well have been regarded as virtually inevitable—though extremely undesirable—in the literary context of the ancient world. That is to say, the earliest interpreters of the Bible very probably attributed the textual maculations that they noticed to human weakness, and not to any flaw in revelation. By analogy, we may propose that the canonizers themselves were also aware of textual maculation and, like the rabbis after them, were not troubled theologically by such textual flaws. Their task was to forge a single book out of different and sometimes contradictory strands. They could not have failed to notice inconsistencies in their final product.

Nevertheless, this text, with all its problems, is evidently the selfsame Torah that was placed before the people of Israel upon their return from exile and that served to unite them on a course of religious zeal and actual observance. Given the maculations of the text and given the evidence of adherence in postexilic Israel to authoritative religious instruction, it follows that a tradition beyond the written word must have guided the people and their leadership in the practice of their law. Intrabiblical evidence demonstrates that conflicts in the written law were addressed and that divergences of the text from authoritative tradition were recognized and in some cases even demarcated. Nevertheless, the very circle of editors and leaders who both compiled the written law and instructed the nation in practical observance at the same time elevated the maculated text to a status beyond correction. The written word served as the concrete symbol of revelation—perfect, awe-inspiring, and beyond reproach.

2

Overcoming Maculation

The Emergence of Exegesis

According to the reading I am offering, the purpose of Ezra's mission was to give the people of the renascent land of Israel a sacred and covenantal law by which to live and build. We have concluded that Ezra and his entourage imparted to the people religious laws that were unequivocal and practicable. At the same time, the tangible symbol of this law, the book of the Torah that Ezra and his scribes provided to the people was maculate and inconsistent, incorporating the divergent voices of its compiled scriptural components. Without entering the debate concerning the provenance of these several textual strata, I began the argument with the fact that the scriptures had been compiled and interwoven in a canonical whole by the time of the return from Babylonian captivity (during the fifth century B.C.E.). In Chapter 1 it was contended that the school of Ezra was able to promote coherent and practicable laws in spite of the maculations of this composite canon. Yet the scribes did not use their influence to change the written word. For these leaders, and for the people at large, the actual words of the Torah were inviolable, their inviolability reflecting the holiness of revelation. Consequently, instead of emendation, the scribes and teachers of Israel resorted to other means to overcome the maculation of their scriptures.

It is to be assumed that the composite nature of the written Torah was a fact known to the earliest leaders of Israel after the return from Babylon. Some residual memory of the canon's compilation remained even in early rabbinic times. Bamidbar Rabbah (and parallel sources), as quoted in Chapter 1, explicitly alludes to Ezra's editorial prerogative, imputing to him the choice of including or excluding certain passages. Moreover, the Talmud, in Rabbi Yose's name, mentions Ezra in the same breath as Moses as a prophet worthy of receiving the Torah from God. Ezra and his entourage of scribes were aware of the Pentateuch's composite nature because they themselves were either its compilers or the immediate heirs to those who accomplished the task. The various strands of scriptural tradition had been gathered and guarded for ages by the predecessors of Ezra's entourage. These leaders of the return from exile themselves maintained the scriptures as a sacred and inviolable trust. Yet Ezra and his fellow scribes were faced with a blessing and a dilemma that their ancestors had not encountered. The people of Israel were now desirous of their Torah, and practical guidelines were required.

Ezra and his fellow leaders must have been aware that the scriptural Torah was an uneven and composite text—sacred and inviolable as the tangible sign of revelation, but in need of emendations and additions when brought to the realm of practice. Ezra and the leaders who stood with him at the Water Gate, interpreting the Torah for the nation, did not canonize the written word alone. These teachers also imparted a fledgling canon of oral law through their instructions to the people. The unwritten guidelines, by means of which Ezra and his circle overcame the inconsistencies of the written word, were the antecedents of an ever expanding network of oral tradition. That tradition was eventually spun around the written canon so carefully that the maculation of the scriptures slipped ever further from the Jewish mind, until critical scholarship cut straight through the webbings of the ages to scrutinize the text beneath.

The few passages in rabbinic lore that allude to the compilation of the canon are precious rarities, and even those are encompassed by furious rebuttals and ingenious apologies. Throughout the ages, the tendency in Jewish thought has been to suppress the memory of canonization. Yet it must be stressed that this tendency arises, not from any desire to willfully mislead, but out of commitment to the concept of the Torah's holiness and perfection. Even as Ezra and his scribes taught rules that, in effect, emended the actual wording of the scriptures, they simultaneously elevated the written canon to a status beyond suspicion. Only Ezra's generation could have introduced the *eser nekudot,* the points that mark some suspect passages in the scriptures. After Ezra's time, even this liberty of near-emendation would have smacked of utter blasphemy. Once the written Pentateuch had been accepted by the people as the authentic Torah of Moses from Sinai, no mention of its maculation could be tolerated. Therefore, in the protorabbinic psyche that emerged almost immediately, scriptural maculation ceased to exist as such. An alternative accounting for the inconsistencies of the Pentateuch arose after the acceptance of the scriptures by the people at large; perhaps it had been held even by the canonizing scribes themselves. In any case, soon after oral guidelines that were not evident in the literal surface of the written Torah had been imparted, the predominating viewpoint held that those additions and corrections emanated from the deeper levels of the text itself.

All, even the most traditional, scholars agree that the literal content of the scriptures is insufficient, and sometimes confounding, as a basis for religious life. The text requires, not only exposition, but effective correction as well, to be functional in the realm of practice. At the same time, it is clear that as soon as the scriptural canon left the hands of its compilers, it became the most holy possession of the people. The written Torah was appropriated by the people of Israel as the most sacred treasure; and whatever its purveyors, the scribes, may have known about the book, to the people at large its absolute perfection was self-evident. The notion of maculate holy writ is religiously unpalatable. It is much more tolerable for faith to account in other ways for the idiosyncrasies of the written word than to attribute them to the vicissitudes of human transmission. Consequently, as soon as corrective and expository traditions that superseded and even contravened the written word in practice were received by the people, the idea arose that these instructions emanated from the Holy Scriptures themselves.

To understand this leap of faith we must remember that for the people at large—and probably for their leaders as well—the written Torah was no longer a document with an acknowledged trace of human involvement. Even the compilers of the canon themselves may sometimes have turned away from seeing the inconsistencies of the scriptures as maculations in the strictest sense. The example of the Passover sacrifice in Chronicles, which I have cited several times, attests to a very early effort, not only to overcome the contradictions of the text, but also to insist that the contradictions do not actually exist as such. The passage in the Chronicles that speaks of the Passover offering's having been "cooked in the fire" implies that the roasting in flame, mandated by Exodus, is somehow embedded in the true meaning of *bshl* in Deuteronomy. Similarly, when the Chronicler listed the bulls separately from the lambs and kids, implying that they were used for different ritual purposes, he was, in effect, interpreting the commandment of Deuteronomy, "You shall sacrifice the Passover offering to the Lord your God from the flock or from the herd," in the same manner as the rabbis who would follow him, maintaining that the herd was used for a supplementary *chagigah* celebration and not for the Passover sacrifice itself. This forced reading brought the verse from Deuteronomy into consonance with the unequivocal instruction of Exodus that the flock alone was acceptable in the offering. The oral supervention of the laws in Deuteronomy was no longer seen as a corrective measure imposed from without. Rather it was held to emanate from the deeper levels of the text itself.

From our perspective in the modern age, we may regard such exegesis as contrived and conclusion driven. It would never have occurred to an interpreter to have explained the *bshl* of the Passover rite in Deuteronomy in a manner excluding its literal connotation of boiling, had it not been for the roasting required by Exodus. This choice between the two passages itself rests on an oral tradition that specifies which verse must be followed to the letter and which must be explained away. All such interpretations must begin with inconsistent scriptures and arrive, by whatever means, at a harmony consistent with the oral law. From the modern perspective, such readings may seem forced. For those who became its proponents, however, this mode of interpretation was a religious necessity, which justified and gave reverence to the written text.

Following canonization, corrective oral laws were eventually internalized by the scriptures themselves. "An eye for an eye" was no longer a blemish in the text, but a verse whose true meaning was pecuniary compensation, as required by oral law. In fact, the recasting of external oral laws as exegesis follows from the aim of canonization itself. The acceptance of the scriptures as holy writ in Israel was founded on the desire to recognize and appease the God of Abraham by embracing the tangible evidence of divine will. Whatever the people were required to do, the written Torah was the sign of it. Canonization provided a visible banner under which the people could unite. Clearly, Ezra and his circle provided additional instruction to translate zeal into action. It was not long, however, before the faithful began to adduce every part of their tradition from the banner of the written text itself.

The very forces that inspired canonization also drove the people to forget the composite nature of the written Torah. In the course of time, the recollection that the text had come from several sources disappeared and even the notion that external correctives had been required vanished as well. Maculations challenged sanctity and therefore had to be excluded from belief when the text was elevated as divine. The scriptural Torah began to stand on its own, whole and complete in the mind of its exegetes, containing all that had to be known. One needed only to look hard enough. It may in fact be an axiom of canonization that to the extent to which a text becomes holy, its origins become obscured. The more sanctified the scriptures became, the more they shed their history of compilation. To the nation at large, a composite canon was incongruous with holiness. A holy text ought to be smooth, free of blemish; its indispensable instructions should emanate from within. Of course, the very existence of oral law militates against the notion of scriptural self-sufficiency. But when oral law is made to appear dependent on the scriptures, this tension dissipates.

Still, a distinction may be drawn between an oral law that exposits a text and one that mends a text or elevates one passage over another. It is the latter kind whose external provenance will be denied most vehemently when a text is sanctified. Corrective traditions imply the presence of flaws to be corrected unless the corrections come from within, in which case the premise of perfection is restored. Expository oral traditions, adding to the written word, would likewise be internalized; but expansions on scriptural laws do not belie the holiness of the texts upon which they are based.

Once the written word was canonized—that is to say, once the scriptures were fixed in form and sacred in popular opinion—the religious leadership, the scribes and their successors, began to believe in earnest that all laws to be observed had their origins in the written text itself. Generations of exegetes maintained that the scriptural word was capable on its own of giving rise to a body of law that once had been viewed as strictly oral tradition (and that, as we shall see, was later to be regarded in just that way again). Correspondingly, if the composite nature of the scriptures had ever been acknowledged, its history of compilation evaporated in the heat of exegesis.

An Analogy to the Babylonian Talmud

As in Chapter 1, we may draw an instructive analogy within Judaism from the rabbinic tradition. The Babylonian Talmud, which took its present form in the sixth century C.E., is a vast and variegated representation of discussions and disputes, which are portrayed as the interacting opinions of the many rabbis cited in the text. On the surface, the Talmud reads as though these interchanges were recorded, line by line, just as they took place. The critical scholar, however, recognizes that the structure and content of the Talmud is actually an intricate construction that interweaves multiple lines of thought according to traditional lore and inherited information. In the Talmud, rabbinic voices belonging to several separate generations and locales may interact in one single discussion, as though the proponents of each represented position actually met in the same room at the same time and were observed by a diligent recorder. The critical undertaking with respect to the Talmud begins with the understanding that the assembled and compiled discourse of the text is, in fact, an elegant, economic, and dramatic editorial technique for representing the many views and opinions that were held by generations of Sages.

In any given Talmudic discussion of an issue, the perspectives of rabbis belonging to separate ages and academies may interact, with intervening editorial tissue lending support or challenging these opinions as they appear. The result is a dialectic pattern that is usually smooth and engaging and that, not surprisingly, came to be regarded, in religious circles, as an actual transcript of events. Criticism, however, must acknowledge that quite often, the named participants on a single Talmudic page could not possibly have interacted as recorded. To the critical scholar it is clear that the editors of the Talmud had only fragmentary information concerning the actual discussions of their predecessors. For the most part, this information consisted of apodictic opinions, which the editors tried to complement with their own contributions, weaving the whole into a format of exchange.

Earlier in this chapter, I proposed a general axiom for any sacred canon: As a document becomes holy, its origins are obscured. The example of the Talmud demonstrates this principle once again. The compilers of the Talmud must have been aware of their own work. These editors surely knew that they were assembling composite disputes, often from scattered individual opinions. In this particular case, the editors (whom I name Stammaim, after the anonymous connective voice of the Talmud, the Stama deGemara) may even have expected that subsequent generations of rabbis would recognize their editorial policies and learn to work along with them.[1] Over time, however (certainly by the time of R. Yehudai Gaon, ca. 760), the composite nature of the Talmud was forgotten. Ever more elaborate schemes of interpretation arose to explain away the evidence of compilation. For traditional readers, the bumps and fissures of the Talmud's surface were smoothed away by layers of commentary, which, increasingly, assumed the text to be an immaculate, original whole. It is not surprising that a work as sprawling as the Talmud contains sufficient evidence of its own compilation to allow study of its textual history. More remarkable is that the work of the Stammaim was so elegant as to allow the composite nature of the text to disappear almost entirely from the religious consciousness.

The analogy to the scriptures should be clear. Over time, the scriptural word was elevated to ever higher levels of supposed perfection. With each elevation, the memory of canonization itself became less palatable until, at last, the actual history of the text seemed impossible, or even absurd, when suggested to the religious mind. By the time several centuries had passed, it had become an article of faith that the Torah, self-evidently, came directly from God in exactly its present form.

Before proceeding to the next evolutionary step in the history of the canon's reception and turning to the phenomenon of exegesis, let me cite an example justifying the assertion that at the time of R. Yehudai Gaon, in the middle of the eighth century, the Talmud was already considered to be a chronologically arranged recording of the actual statements of the Amoraim, with little or no editorial intervention, a view that is challenged by critical scholarship on the basis of examples drawn from every page of the Talmud. This example is technical, but worth the reader's effort, because it illustrates concretely the tendency to suppress the composite nature of a holy text.

The Babylonian Talmud, Baba Metzia 27a, reports, "The scholars [of the academy] asked: Are the *simanim*, the marks used in identifying lost objects, legally valid by biblical or rabbinic law?" (This question has practical implications; a rabbinic law is not considered so absolute as a scriptural one.) Rava, a mid-fourth-century Babylonian scholar, apparently could not resolve this question and considered both possibilities for a while. The Talmudic passage reads:

> If you should resolve that identification marks are not biblically valid, and only rabbinic, then the reason for the rabbis' instituting them as a means of returning lost property is "because one who finds a lost article is pleased that it be returned on the strength of identification marks, so that, should he lose anything, it will likewise be returned to him by means of identification," to which R. Safra [a colleague of Rava] objected: "Can he then confer a benefit upon himself with money that does not belong to him?"

R. Safra then presents another reason. The rest of the discussion is in the anonymous editorial voice of the Talmud—Stammaitic material.

Rava also considered the alternative possibility—that identification marks were of biblical provenance—and said: "[Even if] you should resolve that identification marks are biblically valid, if one cites identification marks, and another brings witnesses, the lost article must be returned to him who has witnesses." In the course of time, Rava arrived at a solution and said: "Identification marks are biblically valid," and substantiated this decision through exposition of Deuteronomy 22:2. The editors of the Talmud, however, in order to strengthen Rava's resolution, incorporated it in a dialogue (which they created) between Rava and R. Safra, with the result that Rava's resolution appears in the Talmud before his preliminary remark, "Should you find that identification marks are biblically valid . . ." The sequence of dicta assembled by the editors is pedagogically motivated and comes at the slight expense of chronology. Historical, chronological accuracy is often subordinated to other concerns in the editorial scheme of the Talmud.

R. Yehudai Gaon, however, writing two hundred years after the Stammaim, took both the dialogue and the sequence of statements as historical fact. Therefore, he commented upon the last statement of Rava (in the codified sequence) with the question: "'Should you resolve . . . ?'—He has already proven that it is biblically valid!" R. Yehudai Gaon explained, "because the proof might be rejected on the basis of what was said above [in the Talmudic passage]." Rava, however, obviously did not consider a rejection on this basis: He had been aware of the objection in question and had arrived at his conclusion nonetheless. R. Yehudai Gaon had no better answer to offer, since he assumed (and believed) that the order of Talmudic passages was always historically accurate, in this case recording Rava's statements in chronological order, whereas the critical scholar knows this not to be the case. R. Yehudai Gaon's commentary demonstrates that a mere two hundred years after the Talmud's redaction, the rabbinic world had either forgotten or denied the circumstances and methods of this editorial project and had elevated the Talmud to such an extent that its idiosyncratic features could no longer be explained in terms of editorial concerns. This one example represents a greater trend that, by analogy, bears on our discussion of the Pentateuch. Over time, the realities of the Talmud's redaction were displaced by notions of preternatural perfection, even though the statements and editorial policies of the Talmud were of rabbinic provenance. How much more was a history of compilation displaced in the case of the scriptures, whose own narrative told of divine and Sinaitic origins!

Exegesis on the Rise

The Tannaitic Period

With each successive generation, the written word became the supposed source of more and more tradition, which was now adduced through exegesis. The scriptures were regarded as God's essential and all-encompassing legacy to Israel. If Israel held by detailed traditional laws, the early rabbis reasoned, then the basis of these guidelines must be scrutable in the holy written word itself. At the same time, some laws that had once been taught as pure oral tradition—attributed to the instructions of Moses himself at Sinai—were now subordinated to other rules that could be adduced from exegesis.

So thorough was the commitment to exegesis in the schools of the earliest rabbis that, eventually, the entire concept of oral law, as an indispensable companion to the written text from the very beginning, was shelved and disregarded. Contrary to what most people would expect, the idea of an oral Torah *(Torah she-be'al-peh)* is hardly mentioned at all in Tannaitic literature—the writings of the earliest rabbis, or Tannaim, leading up to and including the Mishnah, which was compiled around the year 190 C.E. In our own time, as we shall see, numerous traditions, not evident in the literal content of the scriptures, are said to be *"Halakha le-Moshe mi-Sinai"*—oral Torah from Moses at Sinai. However, the idea of an oral law, passed through the ages with the written word, scarcely appears at all in Tannaitic sources.[2]

The concept of oral law appears in two *aggadic* stories, in legend-like accounts of questions posed to the rabbis by a prospective convert to Judaism (B.T. Shabbat 31a) and by a Roman general (*Sifrei Deut.* Piska 351 [p. 408]) and also in the *Sifra* on the pericope *Bechukotai* (at the end of Parasha 2 [p. 112c]). In all of these instances, mention is made of two

Torot, the oral and the written. Paradoxically, the notion of two Torot is challenged by Rabbi Akiba, the father of Tannaitic literature. The celebrated opening of the *Sayings of the Fathers* (Avot), "Moses received Torah from Sinai and passed it on to Joshua, and Joshua to the elders" does not necessarily refer to oral law, despite popular notions. The written Torah itself could very well be the sole subject in this certification of authenticity and reliable transmission.[3]

The Tannaim acknowledged the existence of oral law, received by Moses at Sinai. They could not do otherwise; its tradition was too entrenched for anyone to deny it. Moreover, the Tannaim were well aware that the written word could not have functioned on its own as a living Torah without the sort of definitions, specifications, and guidelines provided by oral law. The Tannaim proclaimed unambiguously that "the Torah, its laws and their details and explanations were given to Moses at Sinai" (*Sifra Bechukotai*, at the end of chapter 8).[4] However, when they grounded their opinions, justified their conclusions, and enforced their decisions, the Tannaim made almost no use of the concept of *Halakha le-Moshe mi-Sinai*.[5] Instead, scriptural verses appear as the bases of Tannaitic halakha (except in those places where logical arguments provide sufficient grounds). Verses are cited, exposited, argued, and employed as the foundations of single opinions or as the sources of disputes. No appeal is made to divine oral information; the latter serves not even as an arbiter of controversies and is ignored entirely. In all the four books of midrashic halakha—where every line is either an exegesis or a part of one—only once (again in the *Sifra,* this time in parashot *Tzav* 11:6 [p. 35a]) is *Halakha le-Moshe mi-Sinai* summoned as a source of halakha (and there too, Rabbi Akiba either denies or ignores it).

In the Tosefta too, *Halakha le-Moshe mi-Sinai* is mentioned only once, in Sukkah 4:1, in connection with the rite of the *arava*, the willow branch, in the priestly ritual of the Sukkot festival. This reference to Mosaic oral law, as the basis of the *arava* and water libation rites of Sukkot, is quoted extensively by the Babylonian and Palestinian Talmudim, where it seems to serve as the basic paradigm of *Halakha le-Moshe mi-Sinai* for the rabbinic generations that followed the Tannaim. It is interesting to note that although in the Tosefta, this view is cited as a majority position, with a dissent by Abba Shaul, who finds a scriptural basis for the *arava,* in the *Sifra* (*Emor* 16:6 [p. 102d]), only Abba Shaul's exegetical opinion appears, with no mention of *Halakha le-Moshe mi-Sinai* or any reference to independent oral law as a basis for the rite.

The Mishnah makes mention of *Halakha le-Moshe mi-Sinai* three times, but in only one place (Peah 2:6) could the reference possibly be meant literally as an actual allusion to historical Mosaic tradition. The other two occurrences must certainly be hyperbole. The one, at the end of Eduyot, is a figurative statement of certainty that the halakha in question (concerning Elijah the prophet) is as reliable as it would be if it had been given explicitly to Moses on Sinai. The other, in Yaddaim 4:3, means simply that the tradition in question is venerable and long-standing. Since the statement in question there concerns the land of Amon and Moab, which, according to tradition, was conquered only after Moses' death, it seems the expression expresses the fact that the tradition is as reliable as it would be *if* it had been given to Moses himself. In fact the phrase, *"kemo shene'emar le-Moshe mi-Sinai"* (as if it were said to Moses at Sinai) is frequently found in the Palestinian Talmud.[6] In Tosefta Challah 1:6 we find, "I swear by the covenant that these things [are as certain as if] they were told on Mount Horev," Rabbi Joshua dissenting. A later version, in the Babylonian Talmud Pesachim 38b, substitutes Sinai for Horev and says, "These are the things that were told to Moses at Sinai," which some Talmudic opinions *(ikka di'ameri)* take as a question, that is: "Are these things *Halakha le-Moshe mi-Sinai* that they require no justification?" The actual rhetorical meaning, in that case, would be, "They are not." A similar explanation fits the words of Rabbi Akiba in Niddah 45a (without the emendation of the Maharam[7] and without the contention of the Stama deGemara—the anonymous, redactional voice of the Talmud—that "Rabbi Akiba made his statement for the purpose of exercising the wits of his students"). Rabbi Akiba, according to this passage, told his students, "Why do you find my ruling [that sexual intercourse with a girl of under three years and a day, if she enjoys the experience, is considered sexual intercourse by law] difficult? Was the law that a girl who has had sexual intercourse while under three years and a day is fit for [marriage to a priest], like all the Torah, handed to Moshe on Sinai that it should not make a difference whether she enjoys it or not? [Such a law was not handed to Moses on Sinai, and it does make a difference.]"

Except for the one possible reference in Peah, the Mishnah never alludes to a historical *Halakha le-Moshe mi-Sinai* as a decisive factor in halakha. The Tannaim did not deny the existence of *Halakha le-Moshe mi-Sinai* or, hypothetically, its power to decide halakha, but they did not avail themselves of it for practical decisions. The Tannaim may have been too enchanted by the possibilities of exegesis to resort to independent and explicit oral law, or they may have felt that the reliability of oral traditions had been tarnished over time and ought to be replaced with arguments from the scriptures.

Let me also note that the Babylonian Talmud (Megillah 24b and Menachot 35a) quotes a source preceded by the words *Tana* or *Tanya*—a designation indicating Tannaitic provenance—that it was revealed to Moses at Sinai that phylacteries should be square. However, the labeling of this source as Tannaitic is probably of post-Talmudic origin,[8] so that we have no contemporary Tannaitic source attesting to this *Halakha le-Moshe mi-Sinai*.

The Amoraic Period: The Rise of Halakha le-Moshe mi-Sinai

With the Amoraim (the generations of rabbis who followed the Tannaim and whose statements are canonized in the Talmudim), the inclination toward *Halakha le-Moshe mi-Sinai* increased. The Talmudim contain many specifications whose source is given as *Halakha le-Moshe mi-Sinai*, most of which deal with phylacteries and their manufacture.[9] It is possible that this Mosaic emphasis was added to encourage the wearing of phylacteries, since the observance of this custom is known to have been lax in Talmudic times and thereafter.[10] The idea that their details were given to Moses on Sinai elevates the importance of phylacteries and would certainly have drawn adherents to the custom.

Both Talmudim also mention, in the name of Rabbi Yochanan, the most prominent Amora of third-century Palestine (P.T. Peah 15b), and in the name of Rav, the most prominent Amora of third-century Babylonia (B.T. Eruvin 4a, Sukkah 5b), that weights and measures *(shiurim)*—the exact amounts constituting forbidden and required quantities—are *Halakha le-Moshe mi-Sinai*. In this instance, *Halakha le-Moshe mi-Sinai* implies an existing definition, specifying exactly the quantities that the Torah intended to be used as minima and maxima in measurements of such things as foodstuffs and in such criteria as the "three years and a day" in the opinion of Rabbi Akiba concerning intercourse (cited above). It should be noted briefly that the source for this definition of age is given in B.T. Niddah 32a as a number derived through scriptural exegesis and in the name of Rava (an Amora) as *hilkhata*, which was understood by the Gemara (Stama deGemara, post-Amoraic) as *Halakha le-Moshe mi-Sinai* (for the Stama deGemara is asking why we need both an oral halakha and a scriptural derivation). This progression is further evidence of a trend toward the concept of *Halakha le-Moshe mi-Sinai* in the Amoraic age.

It is noteworthy that in connection with the *shiurim*, three different ascriptions are offered. Rav is quoted as saying (B.T. Erubin 4a, Sukkah 5b) that the measurements were given to Moses at Sinai, which the Gemara interprets to mean "they are only traditional laws *(hilkhata)* for which the rabbis have found scriptural support *(asmakhta)* in scriptures." However, in a parallel source (B.T. Berakhot 41a-b), the Gemara concludes that they are only *rabbinic* laws (not *hilkhata*),[11] and that the verses are mere support. All three ascriptions imply the same thing: "Moses on Sinai" connotes here the written Torah. The rabbis—or "tradition"—determined that when the Torah forbade a certain food, it forbade it in a certain quantity.

Less than that quantity, the Torah would not call "eating." This determination, then, does not impute extra laws to the Torah, but merely elucidates the terms of existing ones.

Most striking, however, is the number of early Palestinian Amoraim (students of R. Judah the Prince, anthologizer of the Mishnah) who declare that the whole Torah, in all of its aspects, was given to Moses at Sinai. The three most outstanding formulations of this position, which illustrate what is meant by the "whole Torah," are as follows:

> R. Levi said in the name of R. Shimon ben Lakish, What is the meaning of the verse (Ex. 24:12), "And I will give you the tablets of stone and the Law and the commandment which I have written that you shall teach them"? "Tablets of Stone"—these are the ten commandments; "the Law"—this is the Pentateuch; "the commandment"—this is Mishnah;[12] "which I have written"—this is the prophets[13] and the hagiographa; "that you shall teach them"—this is the Talmud. It teaches us that all of these were given to Moses at Sinai. (B.T. Berakhot 5a)

This passage is clear in its statement that all the traditions it mentions were given to Moses at Sinai, not necessarily in the proper order (the Mishnah before the prophets and hagiographa), but all-inclusive. In this view, all extant sacred literature was given to Moses on Sinai.

> R. Hiyya bar Abba said in the name of R. Yochanan: What is the meaning of the verse (Deut. 9:10) "and on them was written according to all the words which the Lord spoke with you in the Mount"? It teaches us that the Holy One, blessed be He, showed Moses the minutiae of the Torah and the minutiae of the scribes and the innovations which would be introduced by the scribes, and what are these? The reading of the Megillah. (B.T. Megillah 19b)

I am not certain that the end of this passage: "and what are these? The reading of the Megillah," is part of R. Yochanan's opinion. The Aramaic indicates that it is a later addition. (See also Shevuoth 39a.) Either way, this statement comes close to the idea that the entire oral law was given to Moses on Sinai. In this view, again, not only the written text, but also the interpretations offered by the rabbis (the scribes), were revealed to Moses by God.

P.T. Peah 2:4 (10a) and parallels contain the following passage: "R. Jehoshuah ben Levi says: It is written (Deut. 9:10) 'on them . . . according to all the words which I command thee.'" For orthographic reasons, R. Jehoshuah ben Levi says that the verse implies that scripture, Mishnah, halakhot, Talmud, toseftot, haggadot, and "even what an astute[14] disciple will, in the future, say in the presence of his master" were already communicated to Moses on Sinai. "For it says (Eccl. 1:10), 'Is there a thing whereof it is said: see, this is new?' and the other part of the verse provides the reply to this: 'It has been already.'"

The last of these three cases[15] is the most extreme, for not only sacred literature and interpretations of the scribes, but also what any scholar at any time will innovate (i.e., whatever passes as halakha), was already provided to Moses on Sinai. We may call this view a *maximalistic* position.[16]

These early Amoraim (mostly Palestinian) also extol, compare, and contrast oral law with written law, an activity we do not find among the Tannaim. The more one relies on *Halakha le-Moshe mi-Sinai*, the more one will mention, discuss, and affirm oral law. The written and the oral are linked, in such perspectives, by the common denominator of Sinaitic origins. It is possible to have oral law (as the result of exegesis) without *Halakha le-Moshe mi-Sinai*; it is not possible to have *Halakha le-Moshe mi-Sinai* without the concept of a divine oral law.

Elsewhere,[17] I conjectured that this increasing inclination toward ascribing all oral tradition to *Halakha le-Moshe mi-Sinai* on the part of the early Palestinian Amoraim was motivated by the desire of the students of R. Judah the Prince to enhance the authority of the Mishnah. The Mishnah, unlike the midrashim, is detached from scriptures—recording very little explicit exegesis—and therefore requires a different form of support. This support for the Mishnah's authority was provided by the concept of *Halakha le-Moshe mi-Sinai*. Prior to R. Judah the Prince, the chain of tradition, traced in the first two chapters of *The Sayings of the Fathers*, served as a connecting link between the Mishnah and scriptures (and their divine origins). In the course of time, however, the link became insufficient and the notion that all oral law—including the Mishnah—was given explicitly to Moses on Sinai was advanced.

The Amoraim, however, were more inclined toward employing the concept of *Halakha le-Moshe mi-Sinai* than the Tannaim; and in Palestine (as evidenced by the Palestinian Talmud) the inclination was stronger than in Babylonia (as evidenced by the Babylonian Talmud). The Palestinian Talmud (Shevuoth 33a and Sukkah, at the beginning of chapter 4) perhaps expresses this difference best when it contrasts R. Yochanan's (Amoraic) statements that the *arava* rite is *Halakha le-Moshe mi-Sinai* with Abba Shaul's (Tannaitic) exegetical exposition of the same rite; it also contrasts R. Yochanan's (Amoraic) claim that the water libation of Sukkot is *Halakha le-Moshe mi-Sinai* with R. Akiba's (Tannaitic) deduction of the same ritual from an extra letter in the scriptures. The Palestinian Talmud adds that the Amora, R. Yochanan, disagrees with Abba Shaul and with R. Akiba, the Tannaim. This disagreement reflects a general difference of perspective with respect to *Halakha le-Moshe mi-Sinai*, with R. Yochanan appearing much more compelled by the concept than the Tannaim seem to have been. (Similarly, B.T. Moed Katan 3a quotes R. Yochanan saying that "the laws of the ten saplings were given to Moses at Sinai," in contrast to R. Akiba, who says that the basis of these laws is found in scripture.) Compare also B.T. Yoma 80a: "R. Yochanan said: Standard weights and measures and penalties are fixed by laws given to Moses at Sinai." The Babylonian Talmud then quotes a *baraita* (an extra-Mishnaic Tannaitic source) that says, in the name of *acherim* (others), that the court of Jabetz (i.e., Othaniel, son of Kenaz; see Judges 3:9) fixed the standards. However, in an exceptional case in P.T. Megillah 71d, the situation is reversed. R. Matya ben Charash (the Tanna) says that *manzapach* (the shapes of the letters *mem, nun, tzadi, pei, and kaf*) were given to Moses at Sinai, whereas the Amoraim cited there (and in B.T. Shabbat 104a, Megillah 2b) say that these forms were declared by the "watchmen" (the prophets).

The *Mekhilta*, at the beginning of *Vayakhel*, quotes Rabbi as expositing the scriptural phrase "and said to them, These are the words" (Ex. 35:1), saying, "these are the laws about the thirty-nine categories of work prohibited on the Sabbath, which Moses gave them orally [as his own explanation of the meaning of 'work']." When the same statement of Rabbi is quoted in B.T. Shabbat 97b, according to the language employed there, the thirty-nine categories of work were given to Moses at Sinai (by God). Perhaps the supposition, in the Babylonian Talmud, is that Moses' oral communication to the people was also received by revelation. In any case, this change from the *Mekhilta* to the Talmud shows an inclination toward *Halakha le-Moshe mi-Sinai*, even to the point of changing the wording of a Tannaitic statement to make it include more details under the umbrella of Mosaic revelation.

Halakha le-Moshe mi-Sinai
in Palestine and Babylonia

As to the overall difference between Palestine and Babylonia, with regard to the inclination toward *Halakha le-Moshe mi-Sinai*, the following evidence may be cited:

1. The Palestinian Talmud quotes several times,[18] in the name of R. Elazar (a Babylonian-born disciple of R. Yochanan), the view that whenever the Mishnah uses the expression *be'emet* (truthfully) with or without the word *ameru* (they said), it represents a case of *Halakha le-Moshe mi-Sinai*. That is a rather implausible claim, for it would include as *Halakha le-Moshe mi-Sinai* the exception in Mishnah Shabbat 1:3, "A schoolmaster may look where the children are reading [on Friday night, and need not fear that he or the children will adjust the lamp to give a brighter light, thus violating the Sabbath]," even though the prohibition for which this case is an exception is only rabbinic. In fact, some medieval commentators (probably including Maimonides[19]), possibly motivated by R. Elazar's comment,

maintained that even such rabbinic prohibitions were given to Moses at Sinai. Nor is it likely that such a prosaic law as Baba Metzia 4:11, "Truly they said *[be'emet ameru]*: A storekeeper may mix strong wine with weak wine, since this improves it," was given to Moses on Sinai. In connection with this *be'emet,* the Babylonian Talmud (Baba Metzia 60a) cites the principle of R. Elazar (its only appearance in the Babylonian Talmud; the parallel in Shabbat 92b is not found in the manuscripts or in the earlier editions[20]), but in this rendition, R. Elazar says only that *be'emet* implies "halakha," which Rashi correctly interprets to mean undisputed halakha, not necessarily *Halakha le-Moshe mi-Sinai.* According to Rashi, on the Babylonian Talmud, R. Elazar deduces that the Mishnah's combination of *be'emet* and a strong supporting reason (in the case of the shopkeeper's wine, the phrase "since this improves it") provides the compelling factor, indicating that whenever *be'emet* is used, the law is certain, and "you cannot obstruct or hesitate from carrying out this law." Since this case above is the only one in the Mishnah where such a combination occurs, the Babylonian Talmud cites R. Elazar's view only there.

2. The Palestinian Talmud (Megillah 1:9 [71d]) cites the view of Matya ben Charash[21] that *manzapach* is *Halakha le-Moshe mi-Sinai.* In the Babylonian Talmud (Shabbat 104a, Megillah 2b), a similar citation appears, but ascribes *manzapach* to the "watchmen" (*tsofim*; i.e., the prophets), not to Moses at Sinai. Similarly, the Palestinian Talmud (Megillah 70d) states, in the name of Rav, that the Book of Esther was given to Moses on Sinai, whereas the Babylonian Talmud (Megillah 7a) contains no mention of this notion.

3. On R. Yochanan's statement, in Keritot 6b: "Eleven kinds of spices were named to Moses on Sinai," R. Huna (a Babylonian Amora) asks, "Where is the text?" and proceeds to give it. Of the eleven spices, four are mentioned in Exodus (30:34). Possibly, R. Huna understands R. Yochanan's statement that all eleven spices were named to Moses to mean that the remaining seven are deducible from the named four. In any case, R. Huna's question "Where is the text?" and his scriptural citation indicate that he did not feel R. Yochanan's claim could rest on oral information alone. A similar case is found in B.T. Hullin (42a): "The school of R. Ishmael expounded: It is written (Lev. 11:47), 'between the living thing that may be eaten and the living thing that may not be eaten'—here are indicated the eighteen *tereifot* (defects) which were given to Moses on Sinai." This exposition begins with a scriptural verse and ends with *Halakha le-Moshe mi-Sinai.* Moreover, one of the defects—clawing *(derusah)*—is mentioned explicitly in the Torah (Ex. 22:30). Probably, the school of R. Ishmael is saying that the verse in Leviticus tells us that there are other *tereifot* besides clawing (eighteen are cited in the Mishnah Chulin)—but that clawing serves as a paradigm for the others. Like clawing, the other

defects involve serious injury to the animal. *Halakha le-Moshe mi-Sinai*, in this instance, means that the list of details is obtainable through exegesis.[22]

4. The clearest difference, on the subject of *Halakha le-Moshe mi-Sinai*, between a Palestinian and a Babylonian Amora is found in P.T. Orlah 63b (cf. B.T. Kiddushin 38b). The Mishnah, in Orlah 3:9, says that *orlah* (the prohibition of eating the fruit of young trees), outside of Palestine, "is a halakha." What is meant by "halakha"? asked the Amoraim, and they answered: "R. Judah said in Shemuel's name (a Babylonian Amora): It is a law of the country (practiced voluntarily). Ulla said in the name of R. Yochanan (a Palestinian Amora): It is *Halakha le-Moshe mi-Sinai.*"

A related difference, though not pertaining to *Halakha le-Moshe mi-Sinai*, may serve here as an additional example of the discord between Palestine and Babylonia. Pertaining to the famous *aggadah* that thousands of laws were forgotten during the period of mourning for Moses (a *baraita* specifies *kalin vechomerim*, conclusions from minor to major; *gezeirot shavot*, analyses based on similar words; and *dikdukei soferim*, deliberations of the scribes), R. Abahu (a disciple of R. Yochanan, a Palestinian Amora) adds, "Othaniel ben Kenaz (Jos. 15:17) restored them through his dialectics" (B.T. Temurah 16a), whereas R. Judah in the name of Shemuel (a Babylonian Amora) reports only the *baraita*'s *aggadah*: "Three thousand laws were forgotten during the period of mourning for Moses," with the implication that these laws were never restored[23] (B.T. Temurah 15b). Those who attribute a great body of law to *Halakha le-Moshe mi-Sinai* will be more desirous of seeing forgotten laws restored so that the flow of the divine tradition is not interrupted. In contrast, those who are not inclined toward the concept of *Halakha le-Moshe mi-Sinai* do not mind having laws decided by human agencies and can live with the notion that some laws were forgotten and left to such agencies to figure out anew.

The reason for this difference between Babylonia and Palestine is not clear. Perhaps it is connected with what I have concluded elsewhere:[24] namely, that when the Mishnah was introduced in Babylonia by Rav, it was received as an authoritative text without resistance. In its own homeland of Palestine, however, Rabbi's Mishnah encountered opposition from groups of Tannaim who were relatively underrepresented in its pages. The greater need to defend and justify the Mishnah in Palestine may account, in part, for the greater tendency in the Palestinian Talmud toward the concept of *Halakha le-Moshe mi-Sinai*. Paradoxically, more extravagant claims were made for the Mishnah in Palestine, where the anthology encountered greater resistance, whereas in Babylonia, where the Mishnah was accepted without opposition, less presumptuous claims about its roots were made. The desire to bolster the Mishnah's position in Palestine may explain this discrepancy in part.

If the inclination toward *Halakha le-Moshe mi-Sinai* was uneven during the Talmudic period, it was almost uniform and unequivocal in post-Talmudic times, especially after the Middle Ages. The rabbinic scholars who followed the close of the Talmudic period adopted a maximalistic approach, making every law and custom an occasion for the claim of *Halakha le-Moshe mi-Sinai*. Whenever the expressions *"halakha," "halakhot,"* or *"gemiri"* ("they have learned," i.e., "they have a tradition to the effect that . . . ") appear in the text of the Talmud, invariably there will be some commentators who conclude that *Halakha le-Moshe mi-Sinai* is meant; in fact, these expressions may indicate only long-standing (and not-so-long-standing) traditions.

I ought to add that the Stammaim (the anonymous editors of the Talmud)—whose activity is conjectured to have occurred between 427 and 520,[25] after the Amoraim—in several instances explained the words of the Amoraim in a manner that increased the scope of the *Halakha le-Moshe mi-Sinai*. In fact in those instances the wording could be explained differently without such extension of the *Halakha le-Moshe mi-Sinai*. This serves as further proof of the thesis that since the time of the Tannaim, the trend has been toward greater use of *Halakha le-Moshe mi-Sinai*.[26]

Before we move to more examples, the reader should be reminded that the trend toward *Halakha le-Moshe mi-Sinai*—which, as we have seen, began with the early Amoraim and continues, with even greater strength, to the present day—did not proceed uniformly with regard to exegesis. During Amoraic times, reliance on the concept of *Halakha le-Moshe mi-Sinai* did not come at the expense of exegesis (unlike early rabbinic times in which the reverse was the case: Exegesis came at the expense of oral law). Rather, the notion of *Halakha le-Moshe mi-Sinai*, during Amoraic times, went hand in hand with exegesis. Exigetical activity was not forsaken, although the quantity of exegetical exposition produced by the Amoraim was probably less than that of the Tannaim, the students of the great halakhic *darshanim*, R. Ishmael and R. Akiba. This latter remark, however, is less applicable to the early Amoraim. R. Yochanan, for example, produced copious amounts of exegetical material while at the same time being one of the most remarkable early proponents of *Halakha le-Moshe mi-Sinai*. The situation changed, most dramatically, at the time of the Talmud's close.

The Post-Talmudic Period

After the Talmud, exegesis was curtailed, and virtually no new laws appeared that were based upon scriptural exposition.[27] The loss of exegesis as a source of law was balanced by the rise of *Halakha le-Moshe mi-Sinai* as an imputed source of guidance. It would be wrong, however, to say that all exegesis was diminished. Exposition of scriptural verses was no longer the method for arriving at new laws, but exegesis remained a tool for clarifying the scriptural text itself and for endeavors to show that the written Torah was in accord with the rulings that were held to originate in independent oral tradition. It is likely that a profound change had occurred in the concept of revelation by the end of the Talmudic period. When the Tannaim declared, "The Torah, its laws and their details and explanations were given to Moses at Sinai" (*Sifra Bechukotai,* at the end of Parasha 2), they may well have meant that every law that might be exposited from the written text itself had already been revealed by Moses in prophetic foresight. In this case, the statement is an endorsement of exegesis as the means of arriving at all the legal consequences of revelation. By contrast, scholars following the Talmudic age espoused the view that in addition to the scriptures themselves, a vast body of purely oral law, not directly dependent on the written word, had been revealed to Moses. After the Talmud, exegesis was employed in the understanding of the written Torah—its words in their contexts and their meanings. This brand of exegesis flourished in the Middle Ages and, it must be reiterated, was often used to prove that the written Torah was not inconsistent with subsequent rabbinic laws. Laws, however, were no longer adduced from roots within the scriptures. Those laws connected to exegesis in the Talmud were, of course, accepted, but no new laws were added in this fashion. In matters of *pesak*—authoritative rulings—*Halakha le-Moshe mi-Sinai* reigned supreme.

Let us now return to examples showing that beginning with the Amoraim, the tendency of rabbinic thought was toward *Halakha le-Moshe mi-Sinai,* in the sense of independent oral law. This trend has reached its peak in modern times, which is comprehensible as a reaction against reform in Judaism. Initially, however, the move toward *Halakha le-Moshe mi-Sinai* was a reversal of previous rabbinic tendencies. The trend of Tannaitic times was to impute all authoritative law to scriptural sources in an effective move away from external oral law, toward exegesis. As the written Torah had been canonized and was venerated as the book presented to Moses on Sinai, the desire of the age was to demonstrate that all valid laws were deducible from the text itself. Toward the end of the Talmudic period and thereafter, the rabbinic viewpoint came full circle, with existing law—even rules attached to well-known exegetical arguments—being imputed to a separate body of nonscriptural information, revealed explicitly and transmitted faithfully along with the scriptures—*Halakha le-Moshe mi-Sinai.*

The following post-Talmudic examples demonstrate the extent of this re-reversal.

1. Two of the rabbinic books composed after the Talmud, *Seder Tanaim ve-Amoraim*[28] (884–886) and *Halakhot Gedolot* (ca. 850),[29] quote the

statement of R. Elazar, from the Palestinian Talmud, that every *"be'emet"* in the Mishnah represents a law revealed explicitly to Moses on Sinai. Rulings based on this principle were later adhered to by numerous Sages of the Middle Ages who, otherwise, followed the opinions of the Babylonian Talmud. It is puzzling, however, that the two authors mentioned above regard not only *be'emet,* for which they have a source in the Palestinian Talmud, as indicative of tradition imparted at Sinai, but also the terms *"bameh devarim amurim," "eimatai,"* and *"bezeman,"* for which there are no such known sources,[30] in this category.

2. The *aggadic* midrashim, which are both Palestinian and post-Talmudic, are consistently of a maximalistic position and quote frequently (with variations or without naming the sources) the statements of R. Shimon b. Lakish, that the Mishnah and the Talmud[31] (halakha and *aggadah*) were given to Moses on Sinai, and of R. Jehoshuah ben Levi, that the future statements of astute disciples were revealed at that time. R. Chananel (eleventh century), at several points in his commentary on the Talmud, also refers to these statements and seems to espouse them. The author of *Midrash Ha-Gadol* (a thirteenth-century popular Yemenite midrash) adds to the opening line of R. Ishmael's famous summary of the thirteen hermeneutic principles,[32] "they were given to Moses on Sinai."

Let me add that this crucial idea—that the hermeneutic principles were given to Moses on Sinai—is also mentioned by Rashi (1040–1105) (Pesachim 24a, at the beginning; Hullin 116b), as well as by Maimonides (in his introduction to the Mishnah);[33] but they do not attribute this idea to R. Ishmael. It is presented as their own opinion and no proof texts are cited—either because the notion is deemed so obvious (it is the foundation of their concept of the oral law), or because there is no explicit proof. For the hermeneutic principles, they need the support of *Halakha le-Moshe mi-Sinai.* However, Rashi does say something similar in B.T. Baba Metzia 112b. There, the Gemara asks why the rabbis ruled that a hired laborer in litigation with an employer and contending that he has not been paid should swear and receive payment (the general principle being for the employer to swear and not pay). R. Judah says in the name of Shemuel, "Great laws were taught here" (that is, there is a special reason for the unusual ruling). "Are these," the Gemara then asks, "laws as such *(hilkhata)?* They are rabbinic enactments *(takanot)!*"—and the Gemara proceeds to discuss the issue. The question here (and in the manuscript parallel in B.T. Shevuoth 45a) clearly is: Why does R. Judah in the name of Shemuel use the term "great laws," implying a scriptural foundation, when the fact is that the rulings in question are only rabbinic *takanot?* Rashi, in his eagerness to broaden the category of *Halakha le-Moshe mi-Sinai,* saw in every *"hilkhata"* or *"halakha"* a sign of Sinaitic revelation, and he therefore interpreted the Gemara's question to mean, "Are these laws *Halakha le-*

Moshe mi-Sinai? They are rabbinic *takanot!*"[34] Rashi probably was not even aware of how much he himself was reading theology into the discussion.

To provide a sense of the universality that was imputed to Sinaitic revelation, let me quote a complete midrash in Exodus Rabbah 28:6, cited from the Tanhumah:

> "And God Spoke all these words" (Ex. 20:1). R. Yitzhak said: the prophets received from Sinai the messages they were to prophesy to subsequent generations, for Moses told Israel: "but with him that stands here with us this day before the Lord our God, and also with him that is not here with us this day" (Deut. 29:14)—These are the souls that will one day be created, but did not yet exist; yet each received its share of Torah. Isaiah said, "From the time that it was, there I am" (Is. 48:16)—Isaiah said: I was present at the revelation at Sinai whence I received this prophecy, only now "the Lord God hath sent me, and his spirit"—for hitherto no permission was given to him to prophesy. *Not only did the prophets receive their prophecy from Sinai, but also each of the sages that arose in every generation received his wisdom from Sinai.*[35]

The penchant of *aggadic* midrash for attributing the whole of Torah, written and oral, to God and Sinai (with limited or no human intervention) can be seen from a change in the Song of Songs Rabbah (probably unbeknownst to its authors) of a *derasha* found in the *Mekhilta* and in the Sifrei on Deuteronomy. The *Mekhilta* tractate *Bachodesh,* chapter 9, quotes Rabbi's comment on the verse "And the voice of the Lord was heard according to the strength" (Ps. 29:4):

> This is to proclaim the excellence of the Israelites. For when they stood before Mount Sinai to receive the Torah, *they* interpreted, by divine word, as soon as they heard it; for it is said: "He compassed it, he understood it, and he kept it as the apple of his eye" (Deut. 32:10)—meaning, as soon as the word came out, *they* interpreted it.[36]

The *Mekhilta* is clearly saying that the giving of the Torah was by God, but the interpretation was the people's. That is even more clearly stated in the Sifrei on Deuteronomy:

> "He cared for him" (Deut. 32:10)—through the ten commandments. This shows that when the commandments came from the mouth of the Holy One, blessed be He, *Israel* perceived it, acquired wisdom through it and knew what *midrashim* were contained in it, what *halakha* was contained in it, what inferences from minor to major *(kal vahomer)* were contained in it, what analogies *(gezera shava)* were contained in it.[37]

However, in the Song of Songs Rabbah, the *derasha* is changed and reads as if the interpretation too had been given explicitly, with no need for the insight of man:

> "Let him kiss me with the kisses of his mouth" (Song 1:2)—R. Yochanan said: An angel carried the utterances at Mount Sinai from before the Holy One, blessed be He, each one in turn, and brought it to each of the Israelites and said to him, Do you take upon yourself this commandment? So and so many rules are attached to it, so and so many penalties are attached to it, so and so many precautionary measures are attached to it, so and so many precepts and so and so many rulings from minor to major. The Israelite would answer him, Yes. Thereupon, he kissed him on the mouth. The Rabbis, however, say: The commandment itself went to each of the Israelites and said to him, So and so many rules are attached to it [etc.] and he would reply, Yes, yes. And, straightaway, the *commandment* kissed him on the mouth.

Either angels bearing commandments or commandments themselves spoon-feed the people, giving all the details to each. Man, in this view, has no role other than to say, "Yes, yes"; and when he says yes, he merits a kiss. Man contributes no intellectual input, divinely gifted with wisdom or otherwise. How different this view from the Sifrei! There, the people perceive, understand and know the implications of the commandments as they hear them proceed from the mouth of the Holy One, blessed be He. The people, in that view, have means to arrive at these implications and details—the hermeneutic principles, *kal vahomer, gezera shava,* and so on. The people are active participants. Ascribing man's interpretive powers to commandments themselves is, in essence, attributing each derived detail to *Halakha le-Moshe mi-Sinai.* Exegesis is short-changed and a reliance on divine supernatural powers is substituted. That is the hallmark of the Middle Ages and the ages thereafter.

It should also be mentioned here that in the *aggadic* midrashim the notion—rare in Tannaitic literature—that there are two Torot, written and oral, is quite frequent. Let me mention a few instances, drawn from a variety of midrashim: Bereshit Rabbah 64:4; Song of Songs Rabbah 1:5; Pesikta de-Rav Kahana 12:5; Midrash Tehillim 22:25; Midrash Tanchumah, Ekev 10, Re'eh 14. The existence of oral law as separate from the written law was well established.

The Rashba (Erubin 15b) says, in the name of the Rabad (d. 1198), that God revealed to Moses on Sinai the decrees that the rabbis would decree in the future. (Centuries later, the famous R. Jacob of Emden, in the second chapter of his commentary *Lechem Shamayim* on the Mishnah, Terumot, reiterated this view, saying, "Probably all rabbinic decrees are *Halakha le-Moshe mi-Sinai.*") As we have seen, the Rashba's statement in the name of the Rabad is a necessary conclusion from the statement of R. Elazar (according to the Palestinian version) that *"be'emet"* in the Mishnah signifies *Halakha le-Moshe mi-Sinai,* since the *"be'emet"* of Mishnah Shabbat 1:3 comes in the context of a rabbinic prohibition. All those who quote R. Elazar's statement, in the Palestinian version (and there are many, including Maimonides), indirectly subscribe to the Rabad's view, as cited by the Rashba. In a glossa to a manuscript, quoted by R. R. Rabinovicz (*Dikdukei Soferim,* at the end of Erubin 4b), in the name of R. Yitzhak (the Tosafist?), we find that when Moses descended Sinai, at the foot of the mountain he and his court decreed the future rabbinic decrees. These decrees, then, are also attributed to *Halakha le-Moshe mi-Sinai,* though they are presented at the foot of the mountain and not at its summit, and are decreed, not by God directly, but by Moses and his court. According to R. Hai Gaon (d. 1039), the (Babylonian) Talmudic avoidance of even numbers (like two cups, utensils, and so on)—*zugot*—which were believed to invite danger from evil spirits, is also *Halakha le-Moshe mi-Sinai.*

Maimonides, in his commentary to the Mishnah, at the end of *Eduyot,* upholds the literal meaning of *Halakha le-Moshe mi-Sinai,* even though the subject at hand is Elijah the prophet. Maimonides wrote, "When Moses revealed the coming of the Messiah in the Torah [Deut. 30:3–4], he also [orally] notified that before the gathering a man will come who will prepare the world [for the great reform] and that man is Elijah."

Consider also what Maimonides wrote in his dispute with the author of *Halakhot Gedolot,* who numbered certain rabbinic injunctions, such as the lighting of Chanukah lamps, among the 613 commandments. Maimonides, in the beginning of his book on the commandments, raises the possibility that "God told Moses to command us that at the end of our sovereignty certain things will happen in connection with the Greeks such that we shall light Chanukkah lamps." Chronology, as we see in this example, does not necessarily delimit *Halakha le-Moshe mi-Sinai.*

The Ramban (Nachmanedes [1194–1270]), who adopted an extreme maximalistic position on "what reached Moses' ear from the mouth of God," in the introduction to his commentary on the Pentateuch, naturally found the range of *Halakhot le-Moshe mi-Sinai* quite extensive. Here, I shall quote only two examples, both of which are drawn from the Ramban's criticism of Maimonides' *Book of Commandments,* book 1. In the first example, the Ramban bestows on all rabbinic decrees and enactments the mantle of *Halakha le-Moshe mi-Sinai,* saying:

> Since God told Moses on Sinai that the Israelites should take upon themselves the commandments [instructions] of the High Court [Deut. 17:8–13] and they [the members of the court] decreed all these, the decrees are considered as if they were given to Moses on Sinai. The difference with respect to the commandments having been told at Sinai is only that some were explicit and some are implicit.

The other example is perhaps more telling, being more subtle. The B.T. Shevuoth 39a records:

> When [Moses] adjured Israel, he told them "know that [I am adjuring you] according to the mind of the Omnipresent and my mind, as it is said, '. . . with him that stands here with us'" (Deut. 29:14)—and from this we know only that they were adjured concerning the commandments which they received at Sinai. How do we know that they were adjured concerning the commandments which were to be promulgated later, such as the reading of the Megillah? Because it is said, "they confirmed and accepted" (Est. 9:27)—They confirmed what they had long ago accepted.

This Talmudic text does not say that the commandment to read the Megillah was given to Moses at Sinai. It only says that the people at Mount Sinai took upon themselves in general to observe the commandments that would later be decreed—to which a later editor may have added, "such as the reading of the Megillah." The Ramban, however, quotes the passage as if the Talmud said that the reading of the Megillah was given to Moses at Sinai. The Ramban's critics took him to task for this. *Halakha le-Moshe mi-Sinai* being so central to his concept of oral law, the Ramban apparently did not notice that he had changed the wording of the Talmudic quotation, thus extending the sphere of *Halakha le-Moshe mi-Sinai*.

More astonishing is this exhortation by R. Jehudah ha-Chasid (ca. 1200) in *Sefer Chasidim:*[38]

> "Do not remove your neighbor's landmark which the men of old have set" (Deut. 19:14)—[refers to] melodies [that the men of old have instituted]. One should not use the melody designed for Torah for the reading of the Prophets or Hagiographa, or that of the Prophets for the reading of Torah or Hagiographa, or that of Hagiographa for the Torah or the Prophets. Each melody should be used as it was designed, for they were all given to Moses on Sinai, as it is written, "God answered him [Moses] by a voice." (Ex. 19:19)

Melodies too, in this view, were given to Moses on the mountain—different ones for each part of the Bible. R. Ch. J. D. Azulay (d. 1700) was not troubled by the notion that cantillation was revealed to Moses at Sinai. What troubled him (according to his book *Brith Olam,* a commentary on *Sefer Hassidim*) was that as a traveler, he knew that there were "differences in melodies among the lands. Also in pronunciation." R. Jehudah Ha-Chasid must have known that as well. He simply did not balk at including regional custom under the umbrella of *Halakha le-Moshe mi-Sinai*. In short, anything considered holy and revered is a potential *Halakha le-Moshe mi-Sinai*. This, again, is the spirit of the Middle Ages, and thereafter.

Of a different nature, though no less supportive of my thesis that as time went on, there was a greater proclivity for *Halakha le-Moshe mi-Sinai,* is R. Saadya Gaon's (882–942) declaration—against all the evidence in the Mishnah and the Talmud (despite subsequent attempts to find a Talmudic precedent)—that the *Luach,* the fixed calculation of the calendar, was given to Moses on Sinai.[39] According to R. Saadya Gaon, the *Luach* did not originate, as assumed commonly, with R. Hillel the Second, a fourth-century Palestinian scholar. Evidently R. Saadya Gaon made this statement as part of a polemic against the Karaites. This group did not accept rabbinic authority and continued to determine the calendar by the age-old method of watching the so-called birth of the new moon. The fixed *Luach* was the greatest obstacle to the intermingling of the sects, and the Karaites attacked it bitterly. Since the fixed Luach did not have an explicit basis in the Bible, the next best claim for it was *Halakha le-Moshe mi-Sinai,* which, if it did not convince the Karaites (who did not believe in oral law), strengthened the conviction of the rabbinists nonetheless. On this subject, I can do no better than to quote Maimonides' stinging criticism of Saadya in his commentary to the Mishnah (Rosh Hashana 2:7):

> I am surprised at a man [R. Saadya] who denies and debates something that is certain and says that the Jewish calendar is not based on seeing the new moon every month but on a fixed calculation only. . . . I do not think that he really believes in that. His purpose in saying so is to disdain his adversaries [the Karaites] by any means possible, right or wrong, since he had no other release from the pressure of the debate.

In the heat of argument, answering an adversary, R. Saadya sometimes compromises the truth. Yet I wonder whether R. Saadya would have resorted so readily to *Halakha le-Moshe mi-Sinai* if it had not been so much in the air, if it had not been, by then, an accepted mode of justifying standing tradition, a substitute for exegesis. A Tanna, if faced with a similar polemical pressure, would have striven for an exegetical exposition, and not claimed *Halakha le-Moshe mi-Sinai.* It might not have convinced his adversaries, but neither would a claim of *Halakha le-Moshe mi-Sinai* have convinced them. In pre-Talmudic times, resorting to *Halakha le-Moshe mi-Sinai* was as much as to say that no exegetical basis for a viewpoint could be found; and positions presented as pure *Halakha le-Moshe mi-Sinai,* with no substantiating exegesis, were subject to dispute on exegetical grounds in the Tannaitic period,[40] as we have seen. In the time of R. Saadya Gaon, however, *Halakha le-Moshe mi-Sinai* was the ultimate polemical device at a rabbi's disposal.

Paradoxically, Maimonides himself behaved similarly to R. Saadya Gaon when faced with similar pressure. He too succumbed to polemics.

Maimonides, like other scholars of his day (and since), employed the medieval notion of *asmakhta*,[41] which ascribes a law to *Halakha le-Moshe mi-Sinai*, while the exegetical underpinnings of the law are declared to be solely a supplementary support. The Karaites ridiculed and derided rabbinic exegesis as a human contrivance, artificially imposed upon the scriptural text. *Asmakhta* conceded to the Karaites the superficiality of some exegetical exposition. Declaring such expositions to be mere *asmakhta*—addenda, adding perhaps a modicum of additional authority through association with scripture—is an acknowledgment that exegesis on its own, without the concept of *Halakha le-Moshe mi-Sinai*, is inadequate to motivate observance. *Asmakhta* preempts Karaite criticism by distancing rabbinic authority from dependence upon exegesis.

In connection with Maimonides, it should be emphasized that he, unlike R. Saadya, draws a distinction between kinds of laws, some of which are *Halakha le-Moshe mi-Sinai*, and some exegetically derived, though the distinction as to which is which is not clear and caused a flurry of comments. In addition, Maimonides contributed a remarkable polemic flourish all his own. I am referring to the stunning categorical declaration that no one can disagree with a *Halakha le-Moshe mi-Sinai*, that if someone claims possession of *Halakha le-Moshe mi-Sinai*, no one can gainsay him. This declaration caused bewilderment among Maimonides' commentators, giving rise to heights of apology; for there is scarcely a case of imputed *Halakha le-Moshe mi-Sinai* that is not accompanied by dispute in the rabbinic texts that predate the Middle Ages. Either the subjects of such laws or aspects of their implementations are consistently subject to the usual give and take, and disagreement, of rabbinic argument.[42]

Maimonides' clinging to *Halakha le-Moshe mi-Sinai* and making it a perfect entity, resistant to opposition or disagreement, may stem generally from his philosophical attitude regarding the perfection of God and, in particular, from the prevailing defense of Judaism against Christianity and Islam. It was assumed that a perfect God could create only perfect things, and if the Torah had been given to Moses by God, a belief shared also by Christianity and Islam, it could not be changed or abrogated.[43] The weakness of exegesis—its subjective nature and its vulnerability to error—made it intolerable as a basis of law for philosophers of Maimonides' time. There seems to have been a general erosion of confidence in exegesis following the close of the Babylonian Talmud, attested to by the fact that after the Talmud, no new law was adduced directly from scripture and that the inclination toward *Halakha le-Moshe mi-Sinai* affected even scholars not driven by the pressures of argument.

Maimonides and other scholars did not feel that exegesis met the criterion of perfection associated with God. God must have revealed an entire and perfect Torah, all at once. According to this view, the people of Israel, through the prophets and the scholars, managed to retain a completely faithful record of the revelation at Mount Sinai, of God's words to Moses—the authority of which, when summoned, puts an end to all controversy.

A most telling example of evolution in the process of embracing *Halakha le-Moshe mi-Sinai* is the rationale given for the divergence of *keri* and *ketiv*, a subject that we have already explored in the course of this study. According to R. David Kimchi (1160–1235)—the idea was supported by an equally eminent halakhic authority, R. M. Hameiri (1249–1315)—the divergence of orthography and pronunciation arose because of the exile, "when books were lost and misplaced and the wise who knew Torah died."[44] Eventually, the Meiri explained,[45] when the people of the High Synod were unable to determine which version of two was correct, they recorded both—one as *keri* and one as *ketiv*.

R. Y. Abarbanel (1437–1508) challenged this view, arguing:

> How can I believe and bring to my lips that Ezra the Scribe found God's Torah, and the books of the prophets and others who spoke while possessed by the holy spirit, to be faulty and confused. . . . A scroll which has one letter missing is invalid for ritual use! How much the more so [in this interpretation of *keri* and *ketiv*] that letters would be missing. . . . The cardinal belief which the great Rabbi [Maimonides] bequeathed to us in his commentary to the Mishnah [is] to believe that the Torah which we possess is the one that was given to Moses on Sinai without change or variation at all.[46]

Abarbanel therefore suggested that Ezra added a *keri*, or an oral explanation, to those places in which the *ketiv* was unusual in terms of language and context. Ezra, according to Abarbanel, knew that this occasional strangeness concealed high secrets, hidden to the average person, and therefore would not change the text. However, in order to make the reading more palatable to the average person, Ezra introduced the *keri*, which conforms to a greater degree to the conventions of language and context.

A generation later, both of these views—the Radak's and Abarbanel's—were condemned outright by the Radbaz (1480–1574), who wrote angrily:

> Don't believe those [the Radak] who say that Ezra the Scribe and the *soferim* after him corrected blemishes, God forbid. For there were no blemishes. Nor should you listen to those [Abarbanel] who say that *keri* is a commentary added to by the Sages to the concealed text. Don't listen to any of these theories, but be trusting of the Lord your God (Leviticus 18:13) and believe everything which the rabbis of the Talmud said, for everything is *Halakha le-Moshe mi-Sinai*—the *keri* and *ketiv* are *Halakha le-Moshe mi-Sinai*.[47]

Even more outspoken—almost accusing the Radak and Abarbanel of heresy—are the words of the Maharal (d. 1609):

> Unlike that which is said by some who are grammarians [the Radak] and some of the *achronim* [Abarbanel]—it would have been better had their tongues licked dust than for them to have written these opinions . . . and have said things insulting of the prophets . . . as if the prophets did not know language—there is no need to respond to such foolishness—everything was transmitted *Halakha le-Moshe mi-Sinai*.[48]

Thus we see that whereas the earlier medieval commentators were willing to admit accidents of history and transmission into their understanding of the text, later medieval rabbis were appalled by such considerations. To these later commentators, everything connected with the canon was law from Moses at Sinai.[49]

Finally, let me cite some examples of excessive use of *Halakha le-Moshe mi-Sinai* from late- and postmedieval times. In a responsum falsely attributed to R. Sharira Gaon, the author lambasted those who dare to disagree with Geonim, saying that the Geonim sifted through "the whole Talmud and checked every thing that existed since the time of Jehoshuah bin Nun, [transmitted] person to person, *Halakha le-Moshe mi-Sinai*."[50] The author claimed that the words of the Geonim "are the words of the Living God," that "their wisdom and *pilpul* [casuistic reasoning] are what God communicated to Moses." R. Chaim of Volozin (1749–1821) firmly believed that all genuine *pilpul* found in the Talmud and its commentaries, early or late, was given to Moses at Sinai: "Also, when one studies the essentials of Torah and reflects upon them, including the *pilpulim,* [through] all of them, man becomes attached to God, for all of them come from Sinai."[51] In another part of the world, R. Moshe Chagiz (d. ca. 1762) stated unequivocally that "even *pilpul* was given to Moses at Sinai."[52] R. David Halevi (1586–1667), the author of the *Taz*,[53] took for granted that the building of a wooden platform for the king on the "close of the first festival day of the feast of Tabernacles" (Mishnah Sotah 7:8) was *Halakha le-Moshe mi-Sinai*. A century ago, R. Moshe Schick evoked *Halakha le-Moshe mi-Sinai* when he could not contain the clamor of the reformers to dispense with *metzitzah,* the oral drawing of blood in the circumcision rite, or to perform *metzitzah* with an instrument. R. M. Schick resorted to *Halakha le-Moshe mi-Sinai* even though *metzitzah* is explicitly mentioned in the Talmud (Shabbat 133b) as a medical precaution added to the rite. (Use of an instrument, as a better medical precaution, ought therefore to be preferable.[54]) Our own day is not without such phenomena. The zeal to ground religious behavior in revelation produces some startling statements. They should be appreciated for the commitment to tradition that they convey, but the critical scholar must recognize that this commitment is their foundation.[55]

We have thus come full circle. From a time when oral laws were imposed as adjunct instructions, along with the written text, through a period in which all instruction was held to emanate from the text itself, to be discovered through exegesis, to a period in which all extant and venerated religious guidelines are held to have been given as Torah to Moses, along with the scriptures themselves, at Sinai. The early canonizers must have been aware of the composite, and therefore maculate, nature of the scriptures, as evidenced by contradictions, erasures, correctives, and displacements of contextual meaning. Concomitantly, these early religious authorities must have relied on oral tradition to overcome the maculation of the written word and to guide them in matters of practice. This reliance was later abandoned, to a large extent, in favor of exegetical solutions and expositions based on hermeneutic principles. The use of exegesis reached its apex in Tannaitic times, in the *midrashei halakha,* weakened during the Amoraic period (less so among the early Amoraim), and has been all but excluded from rabbinic law making since the Middle Ages, in favor of *Halakha le-Moshe mi-Sinai* and the renewed belief in divine oral instruction along with the revealed written word. Exegesis has retained an expository role, in dispelling the evidence of textual maculation and in providing rich commentaries to the scriptures; but in the realm of law, exegesis has been relegated to the field of *asmakhta*—used, where possible, to prove that the text is in consonance with oral law, but never cited as the means to divine instruction. With the advent of critical scholarship and the renewed recognition of scriptural maculation, history has indeed completed the circle.

3

Revelation Restored:
Theological Consequences

Tradition and Criticism

Even the most conservative scholars concede that the literal surface of the scriptural Torah is such that adjunct nonscriptural traditions are required to enable actual observance. Often such supplementary traditions, in effect, emend the Pentateuchal text; yet this text itself remains intact and inviolable, its canonical and holy status placing it above reproach. The scriptures are sacrosanct; nevertheless, a critical analysis of the written word and of the secondary Torah of oral law, without recourse to apology, reveals that the literal content of the Pentateuch is wanting on its own. I have shown that at times in the history of rabbinic opinion, the supplementary and corrective traditions of the oral law have been held to emanate from the written text itself. Even when such emanations from the text itself are claimed, however, they are posited as such to circumvent a single reality that has come to be taken for a theological impossibility: The Pentateuch itself is maculate.

If religious Jews are to benefit from any part of critical biblical scholarship—if the onslaught of ideas from the academic realm is to be weathered at all—then some theological response must be attached to this new perspective. There are great benefits, as well as dangers, in embracing a critical outlook. My first two chapters have demonstrated that the idiosyncrasies of the Pentateuch itself, as well as the trends and tendencies of rabbinic scholarship, become more comprehensible when traditional understandings are combined with the findings of critical scholarship. Still, however, some theological accounting must be made for these new insights if they are to be assimilated into the religious worldview.

Critical scholarship maintains that the canonical Torah was assembled as a composite work, drawing on several distinct strands of preexisting

Israelite tradition and arriving at its present form in the period of Ezra. This conclusion is functional, not only as a basis for the critical dissection of scriptures, but also as a starting point for an elucidation of Torah based firmly in tradition. Moreover, although the notion of a compilation under Ezra has been occluded and suppressed by the predominant tendencies of rabbinic thought, it is actually in evidence, not only in the Bible itself, but also in rare but persistent strands of rabbinic oral lore. In fact, by relying on the entirely traditional concept of Ezra as the prophet-scribe of the return from exile, we have been able to account for the maculations of the canonical Pentateuch in a way not incompatible with faith. Thus the critical perspective of this book has been adopted not only because of academic expedience, but also because, in my opinion, it is religiously valuable.

At the risk of being repetitious, but because of its seminal importance to my thesis, I shall restate my essential historical postulation. Ezra the Scribe, the last prophetic figure of the Hebrew Bible, and the leader of Israel in the restoration after Babylonian exile, was responsible for presenting a canon of scriptures to the repentant nation, which longed to return to the Torah of Moses. After the nation experienced centuries of chaotic idolatry and syncretism before the exile, and years of absence from the vanquished land, the scriptural tradition of Ezra's day was understandably dilapidated. This textual degeneration may be seen as a direct consequence of Israel's lack of fealty to the original covenant of Sinai. In traditional terms Israel sinned— *Chate'u Yisrael*—and the corruption of the nation afflicted its scriptural trust. Nevertheless, a written textual heritage of some description was extant at the end of exile, preserved and revered as well as humanly possible by a succession of faithful priests and prophets amid the tumult of the ages. That was probably the same elite line whose perseverance in monotheism throughout the ages allowed idolatry to be eradicated in Ezra's time. Ezra was the last of this line, and to him and to his entourage fell the task of presenting the surviving scriptural trust to the people who at long last were prepared to embrace it.

Despite the accumulated maculations of the written word, Ezra and his fellow leaders were able to institute uniform and coherent practice among the returnees from exile. Yet even as they gave instruction, Ezra and his scribes preserved the written word, incorporating in their canon conflicting and otherwise suspect passages, and circumventing such difficulties in practice. In the first place, this preservation of the written word is explained by the fact that the scriptures, maculate as they were, were the holy inheritance of the people. Generations of devotion had brought these texts to the hands of Ezra's leadership, and consequently, those leaders could arrogate few editorial prerogatives. In the second place, the nation itself— once indifferent and even scornful—was now calling out for visible, tangible law. In response, the leaders held up their scriptures, the texts they themselves had inherited as holy, and proclaimed them the Torah of Moses.

A nation thirsting for unity could not tolerate divergences in religious behavior. It was crucial that unequivocal and binding instructions be given. At the same time, craving continuity, the nation would not tolerate editorial tampering with the texts of its inheritance, even if these texts diverged from the binding instructions of the leadership. Therefore, the several textual strands—gathered from the various quarters in which they were considered holy—were preserved, each in its own peculiar form, even as corrective instructions were issued to smooth the textual differences. In short, the intellectual irritations that accompany textual maculation are less irksome than the problems risked by eliminating textual difficulties through scribal intervention, thereby undermining holiness and disturbing links to the past. Uniformity of practice and a sense of common inheritance, embracing all groups despite textual divergences caused by dissimilar histories—these were the guiding concerns of Ezra's canonization. Ezra's work retained the people's Torah, even if that meant canonizing a given law in two or more divergent forms. Such occasional inconsistencies were overcome through oral instruction, fostering unity while preserving holy writ intact. Once the compilation had occurred—once the Book had finally been reintegrated as the property of the entire people, no further emendations were possible. The maculate text was preternaturalized—its problems no longer the domain of scribes, but the domain of exegetes.

Viewed academically, this account of canonization as a religious phenomenon is compelling. For the critical scholar, the tension between scriptural maculation and scriptural sanctity is an elucidating factor in the analysis of biblical and rabbinic literature. The religious Jew, however, is left with one final and most fundamental difficulty. The canonization, as described above, seems almost arbitrary—as though a text, hitherto in flux, was set in stone at one point in time, determined by historical exigencies. The religious Jew may subscribe to *Chate'u Yisrael* and the thesis of textual corruption through national sin; but even as this theological position links the scriptures to Sinai, its concept of degeneration over time seems to compromise the holiness of the present canon. So much in religious Judaism is founded upon the reverence of the scriptures as holy in the absolute. How can a position be proffered that seems to belie this sanctity? Again we must return to the role of Ezra, this time to view the scribe as prophet.

In comparison with other figures named as prophets, Ezra at first seems unremarkable. No great poems or celestial excursions, in the manner of Isaiah and Ezekiel, no political acumen or existential alienation, in the manner of Jeremiah, appear in the biblical story of Ezra. God tells the leader to get himself into the Land, and through this one instruction alone we know Ezra to be a prophet. But this single recorded intervention of God in Ezra's life has far-reaching implications. When Ezra presented the Torah anew to the returned exiles, he did so not only as the scribal heir to a line of faithful but fallible human guardians. Rather, Ezra presented his canon as a prophet charged by God to a congregation freed of idolatry. Ezra was the first and the last prophet to bring God's message—the Torah of Moses—to a receptive audience, united, finally, in the spirit of monotheism. Before Ezra, monotheism was not general in Israel and the people were hostile toward their prophets. After Ezra, according to tradition, there was no further prophecy. The unique situation of Ezra—living and acting at a time in which the people of Israel wrought their greatest revolution, reversing almost seven hundred years of rebellion with their enthusiastic reception of the Torah—makes Ezra so pivotal and his mission so climactic. Ezra's unique position, at the crossroads of Jewish history, lends his canonization its enduring divine imprimatur; moreover, Ezra's own prophetic endorsement of the scriptures assures us of their sanctity despite all maculation.

Out of the Middle Ages

We have seen that in the Middle Ages exegesis—as a means for linking oral traditions with the scriptures—was demoted from its central position. Exegesis was replaced by a doctrine that maintained that all authoritative law had been revealed, word for word, to Moses on Mount Sinai. The religious sensibilities of the Middle Ages required a belief in eternal and unchanging laws, not tainted by the human involvement that inheres in exegesis. The Jewish theology and jurisprudence of those times—contextualized in Christian and Muslim theocracies and challenged by the exclusively scriptural orientation of the Karaites—needed to maintain that the laws of the Jews had always been as they were: a perfect and eternal reflection of divine intent. The very notion that human beings had been required to mine and quarry for God's law, even according to the Sages' principles of exegesis, became religiously intolerable. Religiosity, in the Middle Ages, was an obsession with divine perfection. God's perfection—unchangeable, unchanged—was so prevailing an idea of the times that the notion of a Torah requiring human involvement was precluded on principle alone. Interpretation and exposition were precluded as sources of God's law. All had to have been given at once, and in a manner requiring no further intervention. Supplement, even in the form of exegesis, would have compromised the giving of the Torah, which must have been a perfect act. The universal eternity of detailed oral law became a theological necessity.

Exegesis had lost its cachet, to say the least, as the all-important conduit of divine will into the world of humankind. Yet the Middle Ages is the period of the classical biblical commentators. Rashi, the Rashbam, Ibn Ezra, and the other great Sages, whose words still frame the pages of the standard Jewish Bible, all flourished in these centuries, achieving masterworks of exposition and embellishment. How then can we say that exegesis was in decline?

I have been speaking, throughout, of the religious ideas that surrounded authoritative law and practice. As a device to which such prescriptions could be attributed, exegesis was indeed on the wane. It was no longer acceptable to say that any sacred and inviolable guideline had come into the world through human machinations, even through commentary on scriptures. Hermeneutic derivation of new laws no longer dominated scriptural exposition. Indeed, in post-Talmudic times, reliance on biblical exegesis as a means to new laws disappeared almost entirely. However, the procedural dialectic that, in earlier times, was called a source of true religious law is not the only phenomenon to which the term "exegesis" may be applied. In the Middle Ages a shift occurred in exegesis from *derivation* to *substantiation.*

The Middle Ages stressed perfection in the law of God. First and foremost this perfection required that religious laws be based on explicit utterances of the divine, not on excurses and derivations from inexplicit or enigmatic scriptures. It became axiomatic that the laws to be observed had all been conveyed, verbatim and complete, to Moses on Mount Sinai. If a certain law were not explicitly to be found in the written Torah, then it must have been given orally, but in no less perfect form. Nevertheless, the art of exegesis, honed for centuries before this period, was not lost to the rabbis of the day. For the Sages of the Middle Ages, complex derivations from scriptural passages might provide corroboration of authentic oral laws. Indeed the discovery of such substantiations—called *asmakhta*—was considered an important means of demonstrating the pervasive perfection of God. However, these excurses from the scriptures were regarded, in the Middle Ages, as decorative corroborations of laws whose basis was held to be explicit and unequivocal. This is the means by which the nonscriptural traditions of earlier Rabbinic Judaism were understood by the commentators of the Middle Ages. The Sages of antiquity, according to the notion of *asmakhta,* had not in fact derived new laws, but had instead substantiated eternal ones, which were abiding and authoritative on their own in any case.

At the same time, the scriptures themselves were required to reflect divine perfection; in this requirement exegesis retained its greatest role in the rabbinic world of the Middle Ages. The exegetical tracts of Rashi, Ibn Ezra, and the other great medieval commentators are all engaged in smoothing away the bumps and inconsistencies of the written Torah. Whether by explaining obscure or unique words or enigmatic phrases, or by eliminating contradictions, the great medieval commentaries on the Pentateuch are always concerned to demonstrate that the text is, in fact, perfect (though the commentators often disagree with one another as to just how this perfection is manifest).

So consumed were some rabbinic minds of the time with the charge of seeing the text in all-encompassing perfection that whenever standard halakha collided with the plain contextual meaning of a verse, the *peshat,* the latter was defended in nonlegal commentary, even while the oral halakha was kept in place as well. (That is true of the Rashbam almost always and of Ibn Ezra occasionally, but less so of Rashi.) The doctrine of perfection required that the text as we now have it be self-explanatory (with occasional recourse to parable). Therefore, when the text itself controverted halakha, the apparent meaning of the text required explanation.

As stated, the actual observance of the halakha was not forsaken. The great medieval commentators who were devoted to *peshat* were no less punctilious in their observance than those scholars who interpreted scripture according to halakha and not according to *peshat.* The greatest exegete of the Middle Ages, who explored the apparent suggestions of the text even when these ran against the halakha, was the Rashbam (d. ca. 1158; also known by his first name alone as R. Shemuel), who was also one of the greatest halakhists of the period. One of three brothers (the grandchildren of Rashi), all of whom were great Talmudists (R. Jaacov Tam, considered the greatest Tosafist, was among them), the Rashbam had a particular reputation for observance in extremes, above and beyond that of his brothers, as illustrated by a famous story (quoted by the *Mordechai* at the end of Eruvin). It is told that the Rashbam, walking with his eyes downcast (probably to avoid gazing at women), almost mounted a wagon drawn by an ox and a donkey in tandem. (This *"kilayim"* combination of animals is forbidden by scriptures, and a Jew is forbidden to ride in such a wagon.) R. Tam, seeing his brother on the verge of committing a biblical infraction (apparently R. Tam's eyes were more attentive, but less piously directed), shouted a warning to his brother in rhymed Hebrew ("Lift up your eyes! A donkey and a horse are entering your gaze!"). This story illustrates that the same Rashbam who investigated the apparent meanings of scriptures, the *peshat,* was nonetheless fastidious in his religious observance.

Critical study, we see, need not influence behavior. However, the Rashbam's *peshat*-oriented approach applied only to scriptures. In his study of rabbinic sources, the Rashbam followed the Talmud even when its interpretations diverged from the *peshat* of the Mishnah. Study of the scriptures, as I have explained, was not a means to creating new laws in the Middle Ages. Study of Talmud, however, was. Therefore, whereas the Rashbam allowed his interpretation of scriptures to follow *peshat,* wherever it led, he could not allow himself the same luxury when studying the

Talmud, the fount of definitive law. The immediate source of law being the rabbinic texts, the Rashbam was confident that scriptures could be interpreted with considerable freedom without the risk of deviant behavior. Moreover, there are a few instances in which the nature of the practical law is predicated on a distinction between a commandment explicitly mentioned in the Bible and one deduced from the Bible, but not spelled out explicitly. For example, in connection with the elder who rebels against the ruling of a court, "it is a more serious offense in a judge who gives false direction concerning the rulings of the scribes (the rabbis) than in one whose rulings concern what is written explicitly in the Bible" (Mishnah Sanhedrin, 11:3) The assumption is that what is written explicitly is known to all and a judge's false rulings in these areas can have only a minimal effect. For a rebellious elder to be charged with a capital offense, he must rebel against a law that is not explicitly written in the scriptures, and his "false direction is therefore liable to find followers." The examples in Mishnah Sanhedrin 11:3 are notable:

> If an elder said: There is no obligation to wear phylacteries, so that he transgresses the words of the Law, he is not culpable (for phylacteries are mentioned specifically in the Torah). However, if he said: There should be five (instead of four) partitions [in the phylacteries], so that he adds to (and contradicts) the words of the scribes, he is culpable.

The Rashbam, in his commentary on the Pentateuch, when addressing the verses, "It shall serve for you as a sign on your hand and a reminder between your eyes" (Ex. 13:9) and "bind them for a sign on your hand and let them serve as a frontlet between your eyes" (Deut. 6:8), interprets the scriptures metaphorically, not literally. That is to say, according to the Rashbam's own opinion, there is no explicit instruction in the written Torah concerning the wearing of leather containers holding inscribed parchments. The Rashbam, who certainly wore phylacteries, accepted, I am sure, the dictum of the Mishnah, that if an elder should say, "'There is no obligation to wear phylacteries,' he is not culpable because it transgresses the (explicit) words of the Law." The Rashbam's interpretation of scriptures does not necessarily belie this dictum. The commentary follows the contours of the text; the halakha expresses the will of God. The will of God is sometimes suggested by means other than *peshat*. According to the Rashbam himself, God's will is sometimes indicated by *"yitur lashon"* (extra words or letters or peculiar phrasings). For halakhic purposes, and for halakhic purposes only, a hint may be considered as if it were written in the Torah; and that is the case with the Rashbam's view on phylacteries, although he does not specify the hints that he considers pertinent and leaves us guessing.

In further tomes of nonlegal and expository exegesis, the great scholastic minds of the Middle Ages culled the rabbinic sources of antiquity for expansions and elaborations of biblical narratives and themes, weaving these interpretations into colorful accounts of their own, all aimed at demonstrating the perfect coherence of the written word. Expository exegesis, then, was not diminished in the Middle Ages. In fact, this kind of exegesis soared to new heights of volume and daring as commitment to the concept of divine perfection grew. In these functions, exegesis was alive and well. Nevertheless, exegesis was no longer seen with pride as the progenitor of law, as had been the case in late antiquity. By the same token, many a derivation of practical law by exegetical means had in the Middle Ages to be explained away as mere *asmakhta,* as we have seen. It was no longer tolerable to hold that God might have spoken in obscure and skeletal scriptures, relying on human beings to arrive at the intended meanings. It was not acceptable to say that exegesis might be used to arrive at an authoritative word that had not already been spoken by God.

During the Middle Ages the notion that exegesis could determine divine intent was frowned upon, and yet exegesis was preserved as a means of corroborating divine perfection. The modern scholar, however, must regard even the expository exegesis of the Middle Ages with a critical eye. The student of the contemporary academy recognizes the complex elaborations of medieval rabbis as impressive acts of faith, which cloak and recast the underlying maculations of the text and its divergences from oral law. For the critical scholar, however, these maculations and divergences are inescapable. Modern sensibilities render modern minds unable to claim with integrity that apparent contradictions do not exist as such. The critical scholar is forced to confront the composite Torah; and the critical scholar who remains committed to the sanctity of this Torah must wonder where and how this sanctity abides.

Revelation Restored

The critical, yet religious, scholar may, in fact, be forced into the very perspective from which the scribes of canonization regarded the written word. As I have detailed, the school that compiled and promoted the composite scriptures was well aware of the various maculations of the text. Nevertheless, this school was able to hold this maculate Torah up before the people and pronounce it to be the Torah of God, of Moses and Mount Sinai. Can the modern scholar do the same?

The rabbis of antiquity held that had the Torah not been given to Moses, it would have been given to Ezra. Academically, this statement can be used as evidence of Ezra's important role in bringing the canon of scriptures to Israel. From the perspective of tradition, however, the elevation of Ezra to a status just below that of Moses himself means much more. Ezra lived in a time of great change. If the exodus from Egypt represents Israel's birth as a nation, then the exodus from captivity in Babylon represents the nation's coming of age. The revelation to Moses on Mount Sinai, from the traditional perspective, is the ne plus ultra of God's contact with his people. But the people who stood at the foot of the mountain were far less trustworthy recipients of the Torah than those who stood in the square by the Water Gate to hear the Torah read aloud by Ezra centuries later. When Moses first ascended the mountain, according to the scriptures, the people stood "far off," unprepared to hear the voice of their God. After ages of straying from the path of God—after their bitter repentance in exile—the people gathered close; willing and attentive, they were prepared, finally, for revelation. This was the age in which idolatry ceased in Israel; it was also the end of prophecy. Once the nation had embraced a book, no need remained for the admonitions and the visions of the prophets. Interpretation took the place of revelation.

By turning to Ezra and asking for the Law, as recounted in Nehemiah 9, the people of Israel enacted a return to Sinai; and this time they provoked no shattering of the tablets. Forty days after Sinai, the redeemed people were dancing around their golden calf, saying, "This is the god who brought us out of Egypt." Consequently, their Torah was dashed and scattered among the remnants of the faithful. The weeks after Ezra's reading of the Torah, by contrast, were filled with the obedient observance of the scriptural festivals and fasts. Seams were joined and smoothed into coherent law.

Finally, one more point needs to be considered, a pivotal point in my argument. I must address the ages of unremitting idolatry, undermining revelation and its scriptural record. Why did God allow the people to behave in this fashion? Why did he tolerate this disposition? Since God is all-powerful and just, why were the people of Israel not changed miraculously at Sinai? Why did God not grant them the "new heart" of which the prophets speak? With such a heart, they could only have received and kept the perfect Torah, free of maculation. A similar question was asked by Maimonides in the *Guide of the Perplexed* (3:32), in connection with animal sacrifices, the purpose of which, according to the Rambam, was to wean the people away from idolatry. Why was there this concession to idolatry in God's law? Why did God cater to the people's predilection for these forms and trappings? Why did God not intervene and make the people otherwise?

The answer supplied by Maimonides suits the present quandary as well: Revelation did not change human nature; it merely afforded man an opportunity to change himself. Revelation did not change man into superman, only into a being capable of infinite improvement, religious and moral. Self-improvement takes a long time to achieve. It took the people more than seven hundred years to improve themselves sufficiently to embrace monotheism. God, of course, could have instilled a "new heart" in Israel by divine means and eradicated the predilection for idolatry in an instant. Yet with such a heart, Israel would no longer have been human. The people might not have allowed revelation to dissipate; they might not have stood idly by as the Torah slipped away through their uncareful fingers. Yet Israel would never then have embarked upon the improving journey of the Torah's restoration. In the end, true repentance and self-improvement are more valuable than an artificially instilled resolve. God does not change the nature of man, with whom he was pleased at the time of creation. Israel is forced to find its own way. Though the wounds and scars of the journey remain, the holiness endures as well.

The giving and the receiving of the Torah, according to the Bible itself, were not one and the same event. The revelation of the Torah and its acceptance were separated by ages of negligence and strife. In the desert, despite the people's cry of "we shall do and listen," the appearance of the Torah was followed by idolatry, by apathy and near-fatal inner strife. When the people of Israel congregated once more—at long last and of their own accord—they found, not Moses and the pure and perfect Torah of the wilderness, but Ezra and his composite Torah, made maculate by centuries of human history.

Divine revelation unfolded and completed itself in the time of Ezra, and the written Torah is the result of this unfolding. With Ezra, revelation was completed, prophecy ceased, and the biblical period was concluded. The Pentateuchal text became canonized, and no subsequent changes were tolerated. Maculation was acknowledged intellectually and addressed practically; however, the text constituted an unalterable divine document surrounded by holiness and reverence. Subsequently, anyone who tampers with or belittles the text would be tampering with or belittling the revelation that infuses the total corpus, even those verses that are perceived as maculate. A missing letter anywhere in the scroll renders the whole scroll unfit for public reading. Manasseh's jeering that "Moses had nothing better to write about but 'and Timni was a concubine to Eliphaz'" was rejected with derision by the rabbis (B.T. Sanhedrin 99b). Such passages are as much part of the Torah as *"Shema Yisrael,"*—the heritage and the gateway to the highest spiritual recesses. Yet Ezra, despite his prophetic stature, did not receive the original, immaculate Torah anew, but was forced to contend with the scriptures in his hands and to hope that Elijah (and, according to some sources, Moses himself) someday would approve of his endeavors. The Torah was no longer in Heaven; it had been entrusted to human beings, and no prophet was authorized to refresh it from its source with emendations.

At Sinai, God provided the flames and thunder of revelation, and the people were unable to respond. In Ezra's day the people themselves brought the fire of their zeal to the covenant. Amid these flames of faith, Ezra the Scribe assumed the role of prophet and caused a book to emerge anew from the encounter. Ezra himself, as we have seen, saw his Torah as holy and inviolable, and his confidence, along with the new miracle of the people's repentance and attentiveness, allows us to regard our canonical Torah with confidence as the sign of revelation.

After a long interval of idolatry and tragedy, which began forty days after Sinai itself, Israel finally assumed its God-given role and took hold of its Torah. The act of reception itself together with the prophetic guarantor, Ezra, assures us of the Torah's holy status. Moses received the Torah at Sinai; the people of Israel received a canon in Jerusalem. Upon these scriptures the people set their eyes, as they knew they ought to have done in the wilderness. The people gathered close; they purified themselves in repentance and receptivity. While the people were idol worshippers and syncretists, revelation was not only lost upon them, but incomplete as well. The very essence of the Mosaic covenant is the belief in a unique God, whose will is reflected in the Torah. This belief was absent in the wilderness, but it was present in Ezra's day, and thus the Sinaitic covenant was finally complete. The covenant of Sinai was realized by means of Ezra's canonical Torah; thus Ezra's canon received retroactively a Sinaitic imprimatur. The destiny of the nation began in earnest, and our canonical Torah was born, etched in inviolable holiness—not by fire on tablets of stone, but by faith upon human hearts.

Afterword:
Continuous Revelation

From the insistence on *Halakha le-Moshe mi-Sinai*, and its frequent use (in contrast to its alternative—finding biblical sources through exegesis), one would infer that the later one moves into rabbinic history, the more exclusive the Sinaitic revelation becomes—a onetime event that contained all necessary knowledge, making any subsequent revelations, "minor" or "major," superfluous. However, the concept of "continuous revelation"[1] seems to be implied in the positions of those who maintain a "maximalistic" approach to revelation as well as those who justify changing religious laws. The maximalistic approach is embarrassed by the frequent disagreements *(makhlokot)* found in rabbinic law.[2] If every law was given to Moses on Sinai, "including what an astute student will innovate," a disagreement could occur only through a break in tradition; what was known before was forgotten later—a supposition that does not sit well with a maximalistic attitude. What else might have been forgotten? And how do we know that the final decision complies with the original revelation? Moreover, if the law was already determined (once and for all at Sinai), those who disagreed with it, who held different opinions, were in fact living in sin, acting against God's command—an untenable position, since it would make most Sages sinners.

The only way out of this dilemma is to posit "continuous revelation" and to consider final decisions among rabbinic adversaries (such decisions are often reached) as authentic parts of revelation. In fact, the decision that the law follows the Hillelites, not the Shammaites, was revealed by a *bat kol,* a heavenly voice. Continuous revelation makes revelation complete, but not original—not the revelation of Sinai. Originally—the advocates of the maximalistic approach must contend—revelation had no opinion on matters that were later to arise and to become embroiled in disputes. (Of course, that makes Mosaic revelation incomplete.) Thus, in a dispute either opinion was acceptable in principle and the practical decision was postponed to a later period when, after argumentation, a final decision was reached. That decision then took on the force of revelation (restoring completeness to the latter), and whoever violated it violated revelation as well. "Before the decision to follow the Hillelites was made," says B.T. Erubin 6b (based on the

Tosefta, Sukka 2:3), "whoever wanted to do like the Shammaites, could do so; and whoever wanted to do like the Hillelites, could do so. After the decision, the law was [to do only] like the Hillelites [and included all the attendant punishments for infringement]." Before the law was decided in favor of the Hillelites, revelation had nothing to say on the matter and the decision between the two camps was left to the individual. After the *bat kol,* the law of the Hillelites acquired the status of revelation. Similarly, the content of the Shulchan Aruch, the sixteenth-century code of law composed by R. Joseph Karo, is binding in nature—which was not so before—because it was accepted by the majority of Israel, which bestows upon it the sanctity of revelation.[3]

For opposite reasons, those who tolerate changes in religious law evoke the concept of "continuous revelation" to endow them with religious power similar to that of the ancient Sages, who, in their opinion, also changed laws. Not willing to deny revelation completely—for that would undermine the basis of religion altogether—those who tolerate change claim that each generation determines the content of revelation, which may at times require a canceling of some old laws. That right is given to them because they are also beneficiaries of revelation. Revelation is continuous. The content of revelation, throughout the ages, need not be uniform; indeed it may be contradictory. That is because each generation experiences revelation anew, in line with its religious needs. Since the need changes, so does the content.

Classical rabbinic literature knows not of continuous revelation. Its occasional reference to heavenly interventions, like heavenly voices, holy spirit, and so on, are not decisive in halakhic matters.[4] The normative position of this literature is that various forces, historical (*zechut avot,* "merit of the ancestors"), religious (and perhaps also cosmological), were aligned—in a way that will never repeat itself—to bring about a constellation where God encountered human beings and revealed himself to them. The Torah is the legacy of that encounter, and whatever is required for spiritual instruction and well-being is contained therein, either through oral revelations or through exegesis. That legacy is complete. It needs no further intervention. *Makhlokot* are a sign that its exegetical message is not clear and that there is no oral information on the topic. Even when someone claimed that he had a true *Halakha le-Moshe mi-Sinai,* if that information was not shared by many others, the rabbis were suspicious of its authenticity and did not consider it binding. One had the right to disagree.

According to continuous revelation, as viewed by the maximalists, once the law is decided, the previous contrary opinions have no halakhic standing and cannot be used as a consideration, even when circumstances change. The final decision is "revelatory" and binding. According to the reformers, continuous revelation confers a "revelatory" right to change a law once it is perceived that circumstances have changed. For such believers in continuous revelation, rejected opinions still may be used for leverage in situations in which the previously established law is no longer realizable.

In contrast to both of these views, one may adopt the position that revelation was indeed a single, unique event, endowed with unique power and authority. The Torah of Sinai is the product of this revelation; and the Torah as canonized by Ezra, we have said, is not only the closest possible approximation of this original Torah, after centuries of idolatry, but is also the canon as endorsed by prophetic authority. This Torah serves as the basis and the inspiration for all subsequent decisions of law, and disputes arise, not because of continuous revelation of any kind, but because of the imperfection of human understanding and the lacunae of tradition.

If we do not accept continuous revelation, and do not see the later decisions of *poskim* (halakhic commentators) as endowed with revelatory power, then such decisions have primarily pragmatic value—they foster unified behavior among various constituents. By themselves, these decisions add no new divine dimension to the views they expound. Deciding in favor of one view over another does not affect the revelatory composition, whose source and validation lie solely in the Sinaitic revelation of the Torah (written and oral) and in the interpretation of this revelation. No human act can aspire to that status.

The awareness of maculation in the transmission of the Torah itself, and of consequent difficulties in interpretation, instills a sense of humility, revealing human frailties and weaknesses so great that God's words were tainted by them—and indicates that whatever human beings touch has the potential for corruption. Yet despite the tainting, these words are still the most effective way of becoming closer to God, approaching his presence. We cannot live without these words—there is no spiritual substitute—but while we are living with them, we are keenly aware that we are short of perfect, that along the historical path we have substituted our voice for the divine voice. We are condemned to live this way.

The awareness of maculate text also calls for greater tolerance for the deviant. One ought to live a life avoiding even doubtful pitfalls; but one may not condemn others, let alone hate or persecute them, unless one is sure, beyond all doubt, of one's convictions—and we are rarely granted such assurance.

Notes

"Reflections on Classical Jewish Hermeneutics," whose content overlaps substantially with that of this book, was published in the *Proceedings of the American Academy for Jewish Research, 62,* 1996. The notes there are more detailed than those here. Where more information may be helpful to the specialist, reference is made herein to those notes.

Foreword by Peter Ochs

1. David Weiss Halivni, *Sources and Traditions: A Source Critical Commentary on the Talmud* (Tel Aviv, 1968; Jerusalem: Jewish Theological Seminary, 1975, 1982). This paragraph is drawn from Peter Ochs, Review of David Halivni, *Peshat and Derash, Plain and Applied Meaning in Rabbinic Exegesis, Judaism* (forthcoming).

2. Per hypothesis, he reconstructs the redactional history of the Babylonian Talmud in order to resolve otherwise intractable problems in various Talmudic *sugyot,* or "arguments." His major thesis is that the structure of the *sugyot* and "the anonymous, or *setam* [Stammaitic] portions of the Talmud were the product of a particularly fertile and creative period after Ravina and Rav Ashi and during the years 427–501 C.E." (Irwin Haut, *The Talmud as Law or Literature: An Analysis of David E. Halivni's* Mekorot Umasorot [New York: Bet Sha'ar Press, 1982], p. 6). Halivni argues that the work of the Stammaim is also in need of correction: They had to force some of their explanations and redactions of earlier sources, since often they based their readings on truncated traditions that did not reflect the precise text that earlier sages had before them. Halivni explains that the Stammaim preferred to live with textual *dechukim* (forced interpretations) rather than to deny the consistency of their source material. Halivni believes he serves the spirit and religion of the Stammaim when he proposes ways of improving our understanding of their arguments by proposing additional possibilities, based on textual parallels and variants, which the Stammaim may not have considered. Halivni's judgments about the character and etiology of certain *sugyot* are analogous in their etiology to judgments art historians make about the provenance of newly discovered paintings, or for that matter, that painters themselves make about what to capture in their models or subjects. His judgments depend, in the end, on both cognitive and emotive-spiritual energies: intimate familiarity with the rabbinic literary corpus and a heart enflamed by love of God, love of revealed Torah *(she-be'ichtav),* and equal love of oral Torah *(she-be'al-peh).* There is, finally, a profound sense of responsibility to correct textual error and thus restore the plain sense: as if the rabbinic literary corpus constituted the creation itself, as if that creation were broken, and as if those few with the power to mend the creation must do so at once. These are all qualities Halivni attributes to Ezra.

3. New York: Farrar, Straus and Giroux, 1996.

4. Ibid., pp. 158–164.

5. From a letter to Peter Ochs, March 3, 1997. The original essay is Paul Meyvaert, "Bede, Cassiodorus, and the Codex Amiatinus," *Speculum* 71 (1996): 827–883 at 870f.

6. See, for example, Yehezkiel Kaufmann, *The Religion of Israel, from Its Beginnings to the Babylonian Exile*, trans. and abridged by Moshe Greenberg (New York: Schocken Books, 1972), passim; Moshe Greenberg, "The Vision of Jerusalem in Ezekiel 8–11: A Holistic Interpretation, in *The Divine Helmsman: Lou Silberman Festschrift*, ed. J. L. Crenshaw and S. Sandmel (New York: KTAV, 1980), pp. 143–163; Jon Levinson, *Sinai and Zion, An Entry into the Jewish Bible* (Minneapolis: Winston Press, 1985), passim.

Foreword by Stanley Hauerwas

1. Halivni, of course, is not alone in representing this challenge to Christians. In particular, the work of Michael Wyschogrod and David Novak has made it clear that Christian theologians can no longer accept the splendid isolation implicit in the claim that Jews do not do theology. Or perhaps better put: If Christian theologians accept such isolation, they imperil the very character of Christian theology. For two recent attempts of Christian theologians to engage Jewish theology, see R. Kendall Soulen, *The God of Israel and Christian Theology* (Minneapolis: Fortress Press, 1996), and Scott C. Bader-Saye, "Aristotle or Abraham? Church, Israel, and the Politics of Election," Ph.D. Dissertation, Duke University, 1997.

2. The great work of W. D. Davies stands as a signal witness to this kind of turn in Christian reading. The work of my friend and colleague Richard Hays, in such books as *The Echoes of Scripture in the Letters of Paul* (New Haven: Yale University Press, 1989) and *The Moral Vision of the New Testament: Community, Cross, New Creation* (San Francisco: Harper, 1996), is helping us better understand the significance of such readings. At a more systematic level, the work of Hans Frei and George Lindbeck exemplifies such readings. See in particular George Lindbeck's "The Church," in *Keeping the Faith: Essays to Mark the Centenary of Lux Mundi*, ed. Geoffrey Wainwright (Philadelphia: Fortress Press, 1988), pp. 179–208.

3. Babylonian Talmud, Nedarim 22b, cited in David Halivni, *Peshat and Derash: Plain and Applied Meaning in Rabbinic Exegesis* (New York: Oxford University Press, 1991), p. 137.

4. One of the gifts of historical critical approaches to the Scripture has been its refusal to ignore words. The historian rightly forces us to read passages we might otherwise overlook or ignore. Unfortunately, their "method" is too often freighted with redirected presuppositions that belie its activity.

Introduction

1. Moses Alshakar (1466–1552).

2. Moses Maimonides, *The Guide of the Perplexed*, trans. S. Pines (Chicago: University of Chicago Press, 1963), vol. 2, pp. 327–328.

3. See for example the comment of Rabbi Zvi Hirsch Chajes (Baba Metzia 59b): "I heard that the main reason for the fundamental and basic belief that the Torah will never change is that something that is completely perfect cannot give rise to something different. . . . It is unimaginable that the Torah, which is given by God, could suffer any diminution or change. For God is eternal, so the Torah that comes from God must be eternal." (He is referring to Maimonides, *Guide of the Perplexed,* vol. 2, p. 39.)

4. David Weiss Halivni, *The Book and the Sword: A Life of Learning in the Shadow of Destruction* (New York: Farrar, Straus and Giroux, 1996), p. 96.

Chapter One

1. Jacob Milgrom, trans. *Leviticus: A Translation and Commentary,* Anchor Bible (New York: Doubleday).

2. The books of Ezra and Nehemiah contain quotations from and references to all five books of the Pentateuch. For a list of these references, see Y. Kaufman, *History of the Jewish Religion* (Hebrew) (Jerusalem: Mosad Bialik, and Tel Aviv: Devir, 1960), vol. 1, pp. 213–214, see infra note 37. N. Sarna, in the *Encyclopedia Judaica,* s.v. Bible, p. 823, writes, "It may safely be assumed that the work of final collection, fixing and preservation of the Torah took place in the Babylonian exile (Cf. Ezra 7:14, 25)." He also writes, "The Samaritans already accepted the Mosaic authorship of the Pentateuch. Since hostility toward the Judeans was already acute in Ezra's time and since the Samaritan-Jewish schism could not have taken place much later than this time, it follows that the canonization of the Pentateuch could not then have been a very recent event." Both Sarna and Y. Kaufman (vol. 1, p. 213) noticed that the Chronicler knew both P and D sources. Note, however, that Samaritans also believed that Ezra falsified the Torah (M. Seligsohn and E. N. Adler, "Une Nouvelle Chronique Samaritaine," *Revue des Etudes Juifs,* 1902, p. 202).

3. Sectarians, rather than overlooking Ezra's role, accused him of falsification. See Chava Lazarus-Yafeh, *Intertwined Worlds: Medieval Islam and Bible Criticism* (Princeton: Princeton University Press, 1992), esp. chap. 3.

4. See the Ramban's Introduction to his *Commentary on the Torah,* toward the end. See Rabbi C. B. Chavel, ed. *Commentary on the Torah by Moshe ben Nachman (Nachmanides)* (Jerusalem: Mosad Harav Kook, 1969), p. 4.

5. Seligsohn and Adler, "Une Nouvelle Chronique Samaritaine," p. 202.

6. Even this statement of R. Yose was declared by no less a Sage than R. Azariah de Rossi to be the work of an errant student. De Rossi (who himself was almost excommunicated for heresy) could not brook the notion that Ezra had a hand in the editing of the Pentateuch.

7. In his *Meor Einayim* (chap. 9, p. 232).

8. Feinstein, *Iggerot Moshe, Yoreh Deah*, vol. 3, nos. 114–115. R. Feinstein characterized the passage as spurious and heretical.

9. Dyhernfurt (Germany), 1788.

10. David Weiss Halivni, *Peshat and Derash: Plain and Applied Meaning in Rabbinic Exegesis* (New York: Oxford University Press, 1991), pp. 141–144.

11. See especially Ibn Ezra on Deuteronomy 1:2; but see also Yehudah L. Karinsky, *Mechokekei Yehudah,* in *Karnei Or* (Pietrikov [Poland], 1907). For Rabbi

Judah the Chasid's designation of non-Mosaic scriptural verses, see his *Perushei ha-Torah le-Rabbi Yehuda he-Chasid,* ed. Y. S. Lange (Jerusalem, 1975).

12. Moses Alshakar, Responsum no. 74.

13. David Weiss Halivni, *The Book and the Sword: A Life of Learning in the Shadow of Destruction* (New York: Farrar, Straus and Giroux, 1996), p. 96.

14. J. Bright, *History of Israel,* 3rd ed. (Philadelphia: Westminster Press, 1981), p. 428.

15. E. Qimron and J. Strugnell, *Miksat Maase Hatorah* (Oxford: Clarendon Press, 1994), p. 109.

16. The sectarians did not make a distinction as to the age of the fetus. The rabbis, however, drew a distinction between a fetus eight months old and a fetus of nine months. It is explicitly stated in Mishnah *Chulin* 4:5 that the controversy between R. Meir and the Sages applied only when the fetus was nine months old. In the case of an eight-month-old fetus, even R. Meir agreed that the slaughter of the mother sufficed also for the fetus. For more details, see my "Reflections on Classical Jewish Hermeneutics," *Proceedings of the American Academy for Jewish Research,* 62 (1997), n. 35.

17. Yigael Yadin, *Tefilin from Qumran* (Hebrew and English) (Jerusalem: Israel Exploration Society, 1969).

18. See D. Dimant, "Qumran Sectarian Literature," in *Jewish Writings of the Second Temple,* ed. M. E. Stone (Assen, Neth.: Van Gorcum, 1984), p. 546; idem, "Apocalyptic Texts at Qumran," in *The Community of the Renewed Covenant,* ed. E. Ulrich and J. Vanderkam (Notre Dame, Ind.: University of Notre Dame Press, 1993), p. 198.

19. According to I. Elbogen, *Jewish Liturgy,* trans. R. P. Scheindlin (Philadelphia: Jewish Publication Society, and New York: Jewish Theological Seminary, 1993), pp. 119–120, 190, the central institutions of *ma'amadot* and the public reading of the Torah were instituted in Ezra's time or shortly thereafter, Ezra's assembly and reading of the Torah being the model for the public readings.

20. See note 2.

21. See B. Halpern-Amaru, *Rewriting the Bible* (Valley Forge, Pa.: Trinity Press International, 1995), p. 4 and the literature quoted in the notes there.

22. See L. H. Schiffman, *Reclaiming the Dead Sea Scrolls* (Philadelphia: Jewish Publication Society, 1994), pp. 161–169, where he argues that the Masoretic text "was the dominant type." See also M. Cohen in *Studies in Bible and Exegesis* (Hebrew), ed. U. Simon and M. Goshen (Ramat Gan: Bar Ilan University, 1980), pp. 149, 135ff.

23. *Mekhilta, Bo,* ed. Ch. S. Horovitz (Jerusalem, 1960), p. 13.

24. See my article "The Reception Accorded to Rabbi Judah's Mishnah," in *Jewish and Christian Self-Definition,* ed. J. P. Sanders (Philadelphia: Fortress Press, 1981).

25. Pp. 161–162 in Lauterbach edition.

26. Even such a modern scholar as Adolf Schwartz, the rector of the Viennese Rabbinical Seminary, found it difficult to accept *eiruv parshiot* as Rashi understands it, for religious reasons. See *Monatsschrift für Geschichte und Wissenschaft des Judentums,* 1928, pp. 61ff., and Horovitz, *Mekhilta,* p. 301, n. 4.

27. In addition to the two quoted below, see also B.T. Makot 17b, Sifra Shemini "Aaron lifted his hands . . . and blessed them" (Lev. 9:22) (Weiss edition, p. 45a-b), and also the Ibn Ezra there.

28. R. Y. Horowitz (1560–1630), who followed the more extreme view, writes in his famous book, *Shenei Luchot Habrit* (Jerusalem, 1960), p. 236b: "It does not mean that the passage is not in order and needs transposition, God forbid; only that it looks like it needs transposition, for we lost the wisdom to understand the style and allusion of the verse."

29. Yoma 48a; Baba Batra 111a; Zevachim 25a; and Bechorot 44b (and not Keritot 44b, as it is marked in the *Thesaurus Talmudis,* vol. 9, p. 337).

30. For more information, see *Sefer Keritot,* ed. S. B. and J. M. Sofer (Jerusalem, 1965), pp. 146, 212.

31. For a thorough treatment of *tikkun soferim,* see S. Lieberman, *Hellenism in Jewish Palestine* (Hebrew), 3rd ed. (Jerusalem, 1991), chap. 2, pp. 170–174. To the literature cited there, add also the names quoted by Karinsky, *Mechokekei Yehudah,* Gen. 18:22 (p. 220). In a forthcoming article by Y. Maori, which I have had the privilege of reading, the topic of *tikkun soferim* is thoroughly discussed and addressed.

32. See also the statement of R. Simon's teacher, R. Jehoshuah ben Levi, in Exodus Rabbah 13:1.

Chapter Two

1. I have determined that the majority of the discursive portions of the Talmud, which are overwhelmingly anonymous, ought to be treated as a later commentary, noncontemporaneous with the statements attributed by name to the Sages (Amoraim) of the Talmud. The fact that this discursive matrix is not contemporaneous with the earlier and more carefully preserved rabbinic statements recorded in the Talmud, but is the product of later generations, entitles us to offer alternatives whenever the given explanation or understanding of an earlier statement seems unsatisfactory (either because it does not fit the words of the earlier statement or because it contradicts a parallel source). Whereas the attributed opinions were scrupulously distilled into terse, apodictic statements, which were carefully preserved, and which were intended to serve as authoritative dicta, the discursive material that now connects these statements was not so distilled, not so carefully preserved, and not intended to serve as authoritative pronouncements. The discursive material contains many suggestions and possibilities out of which legal data may be extracted but which by themselves were never meant as final rulings or even tenable positions. Indeed, later generations—probably until the time of R. Hai Gaon (10th–11th century)—felt free to add their own comments to the discursive material (and perhaps also to alter or subtract from this material). Maimonides apparently did not regard the discursive turns of the Talmud as the final word in matters of law. In his famous legal code, the *Mishneh Torah,* he often codifies positions contrary to those that seem to prevail in the argumentation of the Gemara, its "give and take," as this discursive material is traditionally called. Such contradiction can be accounted for only if we understand that Maimonides related to the discursive disputations of the

Talmud, not as a passive spectator, but as almost an active participant, a coworker with the discursive voices of the Talmud, almost a partner in the discussion itself, able to revive, defend, and codify positions over and against opposing arguments. Maimonides evidently recognized the anonymous "give and take" of the Gemara as a guide and a commentary to the earlier Amoraic statements, but he did not interpret this discursive framework, in which the earlier statements were presented and examined, as being itself a closed or final legal code. The discursive material of the Talmud, from its very inception, had goals and ambitions different from those of the concise, apodictic Amoraic statements.

2. See P. Schafer, *Das Dogma von der Mundlichen Torah: Studien zur Geschichte und Theologie des Rabbinischen Judentums* (Leiden: E. J. Brill, 1978), pp. 153–197; J. Neusner, *The Rabbinic Traditions About the Pharisees Before 70* (Leiden: E. J. Brill, 1971), vol. 3, pp. 177–179.

3. See, however, among others, the comments of the Gaon of Vilna to the beginning of the first *mishnah* of Avot, found in the standard edition of the Mishnah published by the brothers and widow Romm, Vilna, ca. 1886.

4. For a more elaborate explanation of this Sifra, and that of the beginning of Behar, see my "From Midrash to Mishnah: Theological Repercussions," in *The Midrashic Imagination*, ed. M. Fishbane (Albany: State University of New York Press, 1992), pp. 27–28.

5. There are several lists, given by different people, of the *Halakhot le-Moshe mi-Sinai*. The most recent is that of Kalman Kahana, in *Cheker Veiyun* (Tel Aviv, 1960), pp. 38–57. Unfortunately, he is excessively apologetic. One ought to consult also the classical Responsum no. 192 of R. Yair Chaim Bachrach (1638–1701). His is more than a list. Its purpose is to show, contrary to Maimonides, that there are disagreements concerning *Halakha le-Moshe mi-Sinai*. See also Y. H. Schor, *Hechalutz*, vol. 2, bk. 4, pp. 29–50 (which would have been most scientifically reliable were it not for Schor's zeal to prove the rabbis of the Talmud wrong, making sometimes almost deliberate mistakes—in *Hechalutz*, bk. 7, p. 149, he almost admits this). A sensible study of *Halakha le-Moshe mi-Sinai*, far from both extremes, is R. Ch. Bieberfeld, *Veeilu Halakhot* (Hebrew and German) (Berlin, 1939). See also S. M. Sofer, *Divrei Soferim* (Jerusalem, 1956), vol. 1, pp. 85c–133d (rather exhaustive, but includes some irrelevant material). Another list is that of R. R. Y. Leon Templu, *Halakha le-Moshe mi-Sinai* (Amsterdam, 1734). I consulted also R. Zvi Hirsch Chajes, *Torat Neviim*, chap. 4, a treatise on the oral law, and reference will be made to him in the course of this study. S. Safrai's article "Halakha le-Moshe mi-Sinai: History or Theology," in *Mehkerei Talmud*, ed. J. Sussman and D. Rosenthal (Jerusalem, 1990), pp. 11–38, opened the modern discussion of *Halakha le-Moshe mi-Sinai* and adds a historical dimension to the subject. R. Menasche Grossberg, *Seder Olam Zuta* (London, 1910), p. 76, n. 13, refers to his book *Chevel Menashe*, where he collected "bundles" of *Halakhot le-Moshe mi-Sinai* (176 of them). A. J. Heschel's *Torah min Hashamayim (The Theology of Ancient Judaism)*(London: Soncino, 1965), particularly vol. 2, pp. 71–98, 229–263, contains very relevant material. I consulted most of these books. They were useful, but because I am writing from the perspective of evolutionary development, I had to organize the material differently.

6. See my "Reflections on Classical Jewish Hermeneutics," *Proceedings of the American Academy for Jewish Research,* 62 (1997), n. 51.

7. R. Meir of Lublin (1558–1616). The emendations are found in the standard Vilna, Romm editions of the Talmud.

8. See my *Sources and Traditions*, "Chagigah" (Jerusalem, Jewish Theological Seminary, 1975), p. 613. Similarly, the word "Tanna," which precedes the phrase, "like a small finger," in B.T. Bechorot 44a, does not guarantee that the phrase is actually Tannaitic, only that somebody later may have thought so. The fact that the phrase is also found in the *Shiur Komah,* a book describing God's physical features (Raziel 38a), is no indication that the *Shiur Komah* too is from Tannaitic times. Scholars debated the book's provenance. Cf. S. Lieberman, *Shkiin* (Jerusalem, 1939) pp. 11–13.

9. See the lists of the *Halakhot le-Moshe mi-Sinai* mentioned in the literature referred to in note 5.

10. Among the first to have noticed this laxity was A. M. Pineles, *Daka shel Torah* (Vienna, 1861), pp. 20–24. See also my *Peshat and Derash: Plain and Applied Meaning in Rabbinic Exegesis* (New York: Oxford University Press, 1991), p. 181, n. 49. Cf. R. Moshe of Coucy (ca. 1240), *Sefer Mitzvot Gadol (SeMaG),* Venice, 1547, at the end of the third positive commandment, p. 96d.

11. See, however, R. R. Rabinowicz, *Dikdukei Soferim,* ad loc. (Munich, 1836), p. 222, n. 4. The Munich manuscript originally had the version we have in the printed edition but was changed later.

12. See "Reflections on Classical Jewish Hermeneutics," n. 58.

13. See Exodus Rabbah 28:6, commenting on Exodus 20:1, "And God spoke all these words." The midrash says, in the name of R. Yitzhak, "The prophets received from Sinai the message they were to prophesy to subsequent generations."

14. The Hebrew is *"vatik,"* a veteran, an astute student. The "even" refers to the disciple: Even what a disciple says, providing he is astute, was already revealed to Moses on Sinai. *The Midrash Hagadol, Deuteronomy,* ed. S. Fish (Jerusalem: Mosad Harav Kook, 1972), p. 175, however, reads, *"talmid tinok"* (fledgling student)—even his sayings were communicated to Moses on Sinai.

15. See "Reflections on Classical Jewish Hermeneutics," n. 61.

16. See my article "From Ancient Israel to Modern Judaism," in *Essays in Honor of Marvin Fox,* ed. J. Neusner (Brown University) (Atlanta: Scholars Press, 1989), vol. 2, pp. 29–49.

17. See my article, "From Midrash to Mishnah," pp. 23–43.

18. Kilaim 2:1 [27d], Terumot 2:1 [41b], Shabbat 1:3 [3b], 10:4 [12b].

19. In his introduction to his commentary on the Mishnah, edited by R. Joseph Capah (Jerusalem: Mosad Harav Kook, 1963), p. 10.

20. It is not clear from where our printed editions (appearing for the first time in Krakow, 1602, see Rabinowicz, *Dikdukei Soferim,* Shabbat 92b) took the statement "It was taught, every *be'emet* is a *Halakha*" (before the *piska* "R. Judah says, So too the letter carriers"). It cannot be attributed to scribal transfer from Baba Metzia, for there the statement is attributed to R. Elazar and begins with the words *"adah amrah"*—from here we can infer. (Since *"le-Moshe mi-Sinai"* is not mentioned, it is not a copy from the Palestinian Talmud.) Perhaps the word *"tana"* (it was taught) here is a dittography of the word *"tana"* that follows and "every be'emet is a Halakha" is a scribal glossa that was originally intended for the second *tana,* and the *piska* "R. Judah said" was then added.

21. In the parallel Palestinian midrashim, where this statement is quoted (see *Midrash Rabbah,* Genesis, ed. J. Theodor and Ch. Albeck [Jerusalem: Wahrmann Books, 1965), p. 10), the name of Matya ben Charash (a Tanna) is not mentioned. The statement is attributed to Amoraim.

22. It should also be added that for an as yet unexplained reason, Amoraim may disagree with the school of R. Ishmael, even though it is Tannaitic. I hope to deal with this problem elsewhere.

23. This is brought out also in the continuation of the discussion in 15b where it says: "Those laws which were forgotten were forgotten, but those that had a tradition were learned like Moses our Teacher. . . . Their heart (their acumen) diminished, but those that had a tradition were learned like Moses our Teacher."

24. "The Reception Accorded to Rabbi Judah's Mishnah," in *Jewish and Christian Self Definition,* ed. J. P. Sanders (Philadelphia: Fortress Press, 1981), p. 210.

25. These dates are taken from my book *Midrash, Mishnah and Gemara* (Cambridge: Harvard University Press, 1986), p. 76. I have since, however, modified the dates downward and believe that 550 may be a more appropriate date for the heyday of Stammaitic activity. I hope to state the reasons in the introduction to my forthcoming volume of *Sources and Traditions* on Baba Metzia and Baba Batra.

26. Readers interested in technical examples may wish to see the first appendix to my article "Reflections on Classical Jewish Hermeneutics."

27. See Y. Gilath, "The Exposition of Biblical Verses in the Post-Talmudic Period," *Studies in the Development of the Halakha* (Ramat Gan: Bar Ilan University Press, 1992), pp. 374–393.

28. Published for the first time by R. Ch. J. Azulay (Chida), *Seim Hagedolim,* Maarechet Sefarim, letter Samech, paragraph 10 (Livornia, 1773). A critical edition was put out by K. Kahana (Frankfurt, 1935).

29. See also *Halakhot Ketzuvot,* attributed to R. Yehudai Gaon, ed. E. Hildesheimer (Jerusalem, 1987) vol. 3, p. 18.

30. Already R. Y. Berlin (ca. 1800) in his glossae to *Mavo Hatalmud,* printed in the Vilna Talmud, after tractate Berachot (p. 47a, n. 3), expressed astonishment at the inclusion of these terms.

31. Chagigah 10b. See also Pesachim 38b and Baba Metzia at the end of 32a.

32. *Midrash Hagadol,* Leviticus, ed. A. Steinsaltz (Jerusalem: Mosad Harav Kook, 1976), p. 17.

33. The Radbaz, Responsum no. 1303, goes even farther and states categorically that just as the thirteen hermeneutic principles of halakha were given to Moses on Sinai, so were the thirty-six (!) hermeneutical principles of *aggadah.*

34. Rashi, in his commentary on the Pentateuch, Genesis 24:5, speaking of the word *"vetorotai"*—my Torot—says "to include the oral law, *Halakha le-Moshe mi-Sinai."* In the sources from which Rashi took his comment (B.T. Yoma 28b, Genesis Rabbah [Theodor Albeck edition, p. 703]), *Halakha le-Moshe mi-Sinai* is not mentioned.

35. Emphasis added. See *Sifrei Deut.* Piska 41 (for parallels, see the Finkelstein edition, p. 86): "Even if one learns an interpretation from the least learned of the Israelites, he should consider it as if he had learned it from Moshe . . . as if he had learned if from the Almighty One." See also Mevo Hatalmud, attributed to Shemuel Hanagid, found in the Vilna Talmud after Tractate Berakhot, p. 46a, and *Midrash Rabbah* on Numbers 13:16.

36. P. 267 in Lauterbach edition. Emphasis added.

37. Ibid., p. 313.

38. No. 817; p. 207 in Wistinetzky's edition.

39. The literature on R. Saadya Gaon's opinion is quite extensive, assembled and discussed by R. M. Kashar, *Torah Shelemah* (New York: Machon Torah Shelemah, 1949), vol. 13, pp. 40–66.

40. See my "Reflections on Classical Jewish Hermeneutics," n. 91.

41. See Halivni, *Peshat and Derash*, pp. 13–16, 155–157, where the history of *asmakhta* is traced. As to Maimonides' distinction between different kinds of laws, for some of which the *derashot* are *asmakhtot* and for some not, see J. Neubauer, *Harambam al Divrei Soferim* (Jerusalem: Mosad Harav Kook, 1954).

42. The first to raise the banner of astonishment was R. Yair Chaim Bachrach (seventeenth century), in his enormously learned book of Responsa, *Chavot Yair,* no. 192. The many defenses offered, including that of R. Zvi Hirsh Chajes, *Torat Neviim,* chapter 4, have not obviated in the least (except perhaps in a few individual instances) R. Bachrach's basic arguments. Maimonides said this for polemical reasons, and not unlike R. Saadya before him, when he engaged in polemic, he conveniently ignored evidence to the contrary.

43. See R. Saadya's *Book of Doctrines and Beliefs,* chapter 3:7–8 (pp. 131–139 in Joseph Capah's translation [Jerusalem: Sura, 1970]) for his arguments against the abrogation of the Torah.

44. R. D. Kimchi, in his introduction to the book of Joshua; 2 Samuel 15:21, 21:10; 1 Kings 17:14.

45. *Kiryat Sefer,* ed. M. Hirshler (Jerusalem, 1956), in the introduction, n. 3. See also the Meiri's commentary to tractate Nedarim, *The Complete Israeli Talmud,* ed. A. Liss (Jerusalem, 1965), p. 150.

46. In his introduction to the book of Jeremiah.

47. Radbaz, Responsum no. 1020.

48. Maharal, *Tiferet Israel,* chap. 66.

49. See also R. M. L. Malbim (1809–1879), introduction to the book of Jeremiah, where he severely criticized Abarbanel's assertion of the stylistic imperfections of the book of Jeremiah (the many *keri* and *ketiv* variants, for example). Instead, he suggests that the *keri* represents the *peshat* and the *ketiv* the *derash*. For a more detailed discussion of the different views of *keri* and *ketiv,* see M. Ben Yitzchak, "Keri and Ketiv," *HaMa'Yan,* a scholarly journal, Nisan 1993, pp. 49–55.

50. *Shaarei Teshuvah*, ed. R. W. Leiter (New York, 1946), Responsum no. 187. Responsum no. 54 states in the name of R. Sharira that "the wisdom of the Geonim and their pilpul is what God spoke to Moses [on Sinai]." There is a famous letter by R. Samuel ben Ali, published by S. Asaf in "A Collection of Letters of Samuel ben Ali and His Generation" (Hebrew), *Tarbiz* 1, 1930, p. 64, in which he claims that "the place of the Yeshiva is the throne of the Torah . . . it is the place that is designed for the study of Torah and its teaching and for the transmission of halakha, generation after generation, until it reaches Moses our teacher. . . . The Yeshiva is the place of Moses our Teacher."

51. *Ruach Chaim,* commenting on the *Sayings of the Fathers* (Avot), on the first *mishnah,* p. 4a, s.v. *hem ameru.*

52. See also R. D. Nito (1654–1728), *Mateh Dan, Sefat Emet* (London, 1713), second debate, p. 5.

53. Orach Chaim, 668, 1.

54. See J. Katz, *HaHalakha beMeitzar* (Jerusalem: Magnes Press, 1992).

55. See "Reflections on Classical Jewish Hermeneutics," n. 105.

Afterword

1. See Isaac Barnays, "Der Biblische Orient," anonymous, 1, pp.32–34; L. Duckes, *Jahrbuch des Jüdisch-Literarischen Gesellschaft*, 1907, p. 310; Isaac Heineman, *Ta'amei Hamitzvot Besifrut Yisrael* (Jerusalem, 1956), vol. 2, pp. 164–166, 280.

2. For the Geonic solution to the problem of *makhlokot,* see M. Zucker, "LeBaayat HaMakhlokot," S. Baron Jubilee Volume (Jerusalem, 1975); S. Abramson, *Sinai*, 88, 1818, pp. 214–215, and my essay "On Man's Role in Revelation," in *From Ancient Israel to Modern Judaism: Essays in Honor of Marvin Fox*, ed. J. Neusner et al. (Brown University, 1980), pp. 36–42.

3. See Y. Spiegel, *Asufot*, 41, ed. M. Benyahu (Jerusalem, 1990), pp. 23ff.

4. See R. Margoliot, *She'elot Uteshuvot min Hashamayim* (Jerusalem, 1957), pp. 25–41.

About the Book and Author

Modern critical scholars divide the Pentateuch into distinct components and constituent strata of tradition, identifying areas of unevenness in the scriptural tradition, which point to several interwoven documents rather than one seamless whole. Although the conclusions reached by such critical scholarship are still matters of dispute, the inconsistencies identified stand clearly before us and pose a serious challenge to the believer in divine revelation. How can a text marred by contradiction be the legacy of Sinai? How can there be reverence for Holy Scriptures that show signs of human intervention? David Weiss Halivni explores these questions, not by disputing the evidence itself or by defending at all costs the absolute integrity of the Pentateuchal words, but rather by accepting the inconsistencies of the text as such and asking how this text might yet be a divine legacy.

Inconsistencies and unevenness in the Pentateuchal scriptures are not the discovery of modern textual science alone. Halivni demonstrates that the earliest stewards of the Torah, including some of those represented in the Bible itself, were aware of discrepancies within the tradition. From the time of the books of Chronicles through that of the rabbinic commentaries, perceptive readers of the scriptures, noticing maculations, which mitigate against the notion of an unblemished, divine document, have responded to them in different ways.

Revelation Restored asserts that acknowledging and accounting for maculation in the Pentateuchal text is not alien to the biblical or rabbinic tradition and need not belie the tradition of revelation. Moreover, Halivni argues that through recognizing textual problems in the scriptures and the efforts to resolve them in tradition, we may learn about not only the nature of the Pentateuch itself but also the continuing relationship between its people and its Source.

David Weiss Halivni is Lucius N. Littauer Professor of Classical Jewish Civilization at Columbia University.

Subject Index

Amoraim, 57, 58, 59, 63, 93(n.1)

Babylonian exile
  and repentance, 12, 83
  return from, 12–15, 19, 83
  and textual problems, 9
  zeal to embrace scriptural Torah in
    period of return from, 13, 19, 23,
    83
Babylonian Talmud
  analogy to scriptures, 51–54
  composition discussed, 51–52
  Stamaim (anonymous editors of the
    Talmud), 52, 63
  dates, 96(n.25)
  treated as commentary, 93(n.1)
  and the word "Tanna", 95(n.8),
    96(n.20)
Bar Kokhba Revolt, 21
Be'emet, 64, 96(n.20)
Be'emet ameru, 60–62
Booths
  building materials, 23
  festival of, 23
Bshl: understood to denote boiling, 25,
  49–50

Calendar (luach), 70
Chagigiah offerings, 25, 26, 49
Christianity, 71, 78

Dead Sea Scrolls, 20, 22
  Qumran sectarians, 92(n.16)

Exegesis
  curtailed after close of Talmud, 63
  demoted during the Middle middle
    ages, 78, 80

derivation vs. substantiation
  (asmakhta), 71, 78, 82
disagreements (machloket), 87, 88,
  98(n.2)
distinction between exposition and
  restoration of a text, 50–51
as a document becomes holy its
  origins are obscured, 52
eiruv parshiot (interweaving of
  sections), 41, 93(n.26)
gorin umosifin vedorshin (one may
  subtract, add and interpret),
  41–42
"If it has no bearing on its own
  subject, apply it elsewhere," 40, 44
kilkul cheshbonot (an error in
  calculation), 7–38, 44
misplacement of a verse, 40
sirus (trasposing order of words), 41
tikkun soferim (an emendation of the
  scribes), 42
yitur lashon (extra words or letters
  or unusual phrasing), 81
Eye for an eye, 7, 50
Ezra (As a central figure in the
  historical analysis and the
  theology of this book, Ezra
  appears almost on every page. The
  following references highlight
  salient roles of Ezra.)
  editorial prerogative of, 3
  leader of return from exile, 10
  likened to Moses, 3, 15, 47, 80
  presenter of Scriptures to the people,
    3, 14, 15, 44–45, 75, 76, 78, 85
  as prophet, 3, 10, 14, 48, 76
  rabbinic recognition of editorial role,
    3, 16, 17, 44–45

Index of Textual References

Halakhic Midrashim

Index of Names

Biblical Figures

Mishnaic and Talmudic Rabbis

Post-Talmudic Rabbis and Modern Scholars

OHAVI ZEDEK SYNAGOGUE LIBRARY
188 NORTH PROSPECT STREET
BURLINGTON, VERMONT 05401
(802) 864-0218

WITHDRAWN